This We Believe . . .
This We Proclaim

This We Believe...
This We Proclaim

By

Earl L. Martin, M.A., D.D.

Warner Press, Inc.
Anderson, Indiana
1971

© **Earl L. Martin**, 1952

All rights reserved. No portion of this book may be reproduced, stored in a retrival system, or transmitted in any form without the expressed written permission of the copyright holder, except for brief quotations in printed reviews.

Perfect Bound
ISBN: **978-1-60416-053-6**
ITEM # **00235**

Trade Cloth
ISBN: **978-1-60416-054-3**
ITEM # **01888**

©1952 Gospel Trumpet Company

©1971 Seventh Printing

Reprinted On Demand 2007
Printed and bound in the United States of America

© 2007 Reformation Publishers
242 University Drive
Prestonsburg, KY 41653
1-800-765-2464
Fax 606-886-7222
rpublisher@aol.com
www.reformationpublishers.com

CONTENTS

CHAPTER	PAGE

I. CONCERNING GOD AND HIS REVELATION OF HIMSELF 7

WHY WE BELIEVE GOD IS: An Intuitive Idea; God Has Revealed Himself; God Left Not Himself Without Witness; The Bible as a Record of God's Revelation

WHAT IS GOD LIKE?: Defining God; The Attributes of God; God as Trinity

THE WORKS OF GOD: In Creation; In Natural Providence; In History

SUMMARY

II. CONCERNING MAN AND HIS PREDICAMENT   27

MAN AS HE WAS MADE: His Origin; His Constitution

MAN AS HE HAS BECOME: The Fall of Man; Man Is Corrupted by Sin; Man as a Sinner; Man Still a Person; Man Is a Free Being; Consequences of Sin

AFFIRMATIONS

III. CONCERNING CHRIST AND HIS REDEMPTIVE WORK 43

CHRIST'S MISSION OF REDEMPTION: Redeemer and Redemption; Christ's Work Is a Redemptive Work

REDEMPTION BY RECONCILIATION: The Good News in Christ; Theories of Atonement; The Fact of Atonement

SON OF GOD, SON OF MAN: In Him We Know God; In Jesus We Know Man

SUMMARY

PAGE

IV. CONCERNING CHRISTIAN EXPERIENCE AND LIFE 59

CHRISTIAN EXPERIENCE: Is an Experience of Christ; Means Salvation; Justification by Faith; Sanctification by the Spirit

MAN'S PART IN BECOMING A CHRISTIAN: Repentance; Faith

THE CHRISTIAN LIFE: A New Way of Life; A Life of Blessedness

SUMMARY

V. CONCERNING THE CHURCH AND ITS MISSION   75

WHAT IS THE CHURCH? The Universal Church; The Local Congregation; Intercongregational and General Co-operation

THE CHURCH AND THE QUEST FOR UNITY: Unity of the Spirit; A Functioning Unity Is Needed

THE MISSION OF THE CHURCH: Is to Edify Its Members; Is the Worship of God; Is to Herald the Evangel

THE CHURCH AND ITS SYMBOLIC CEREMONIES: Baptism; The Lord's Supper; Foot Washing; Symbols May Be Empty Forms

SUMMARY

VI. CONCERNING THE ASSURED HOPE FOR THE FUTURE 95

GOD'S PURPOSE FOR THE INDIVIDUAL ACCOMPLISHED: Faith in the Future; "If a Man Die . . ."; "Shall He Live Again?"

GOD'S PURPOSE FOR THE RACE ACCOMPLISHED: Complete Redemption of the Race; The Church Triumphant; The Consummation of the Kingdom; Christian Eschatology

THE RETURN OF CHRIST: Teaching of the New Testament in General; Jesus' Own Teaching; Blessed Hope of Early Church; Fact and Speculation

WHAT WILL TAKE PLACE AT HIS COMING? The Resurrection; The Judgment; The Fate of the Lost; The Reward of the Saved

SUMMING UP

This We Believe . . . This We Proclaim

Chapter I

CONCERNING GOD AND HIS REVELATION OF HIMSELF

"He that cometh to God must believe that he is, and that he is a rewarder of them that diligently seek him" (Heb. 11:6).

God is. "In the beginning God" (Gen. 1:1). This the Bible proclaims in the very first verse. This and more we truly believe; this and more we joyfully proclaim.

God is that supreme eternal Being upon whom all else that is absolutely depends. He is the Being who alone truly *is*— totally and eternally underived. He is the One without whom nothing else would be, even as someone has put it: "God minus the world equals God; the world minus God equals nothing."

He is the one in whom "we live and move and have our being" (Acts 17:28). The Bible assumes it. Reason demands it. Faith affirms it. Experience proves it. Life demonstrates it. Love shouts it aloud.

God "is a rewarder of them that diligently seek him." God is a God who takes a present personal interest in all that concerns us. The God revealed in Jesus Christ is a God who knows, feels, speaks, listens, loves, and acts; One whom we can know, talk to, listen to, love, worship, serve, obey, and proclaim to the world.

The idea of God and the truth about God are the greatest thoughts of which we are capable. Knowing that this is true, and knowing that all the issues of a man's life are bound up in his concepts of God, we need to consider the words of J. H. Jowett, "The most tremendous thing you can give to others is their idea about God. If you give them a wrong idea, you may blight their lives, but if you give them a right one they may just leap into love at first sight and enjoy Him and what is right to the end of their days."

Furthermore, this we believe and this we proclaim, that God has made and still makes himself known to men. He has revealed himself in many ways. It is his very nature to disclose and manifest himself. It is to this revelation of himself as recorded in the Bible that we shall go for the main materials of our study.

In this first chapter we shall consider: (1) Why we believe God is; (2) What is God like?; (3) The works of God.

Why We Believe God Is

"God is." This truth was introduced in the first paragraph and acceptance of it is the irreducible minimum if man is to find God. The Bible does not attempt to prove the existence of God; it begins by assuming the fact. Reason does not prove God, but there are reasons for believing in God.

Concerning God and His Revelation of Himself

An Intuitive Idea

Man is a believing being. Belief in a higher power or person is intuitive—one of those basic facts of existence. Belief in a power beyond and not of ourselves is basic in human thought. We do not originate the idea of God; we just come upon it. It is there; we cannot in reality and in fact get away from it.

The idea of God is a part of the basic equipment of the race. Man has a capacity for belief in God. This basic belief in a higher power is, in fact, an expression of man's whole nature, which can be but imperfectly rationalized and expressed. Belief arises from the fact that man was made "in the image of God," and God is within as well as without. We come upon Him everywhere, and especially do we meet him within—in consciousness.

God Has Revealed Himself

There is within man that which makes him capable of receiving a revelation of God, of knowing God. It is in the very nature of God to make himself known to man whom he has created with the capacity to know him. God has made himself known to man in the processes of nature, of history, and of experience. This self-disclosure of God is a part of our social inheritance as well as of our personal experience.

God Left Not Himself Without Witness

Life brings to us many evidences that God is. There is much in the world, in history, and in life, which may seem to deny God, but "nevertheless he left not himself without witness, in that he did good, and gave us rain from heaven, and fruitful seasons, filling our hearts with food and gladness" (Acts 14:17). Again

Romans 1:20 reminds us, "For the invisible things of him from the creation of the world are clearly seen, being understood by the things that are made, even his eternal power and Godhead; so that they are without excuse." And if *they* were without excuse, how much more *we*, living as we do in this dispensation of light.

The universe witnesses to Him. Everywhere in nature you will find God. Look at the world, with its law and order, and you will have to admit that there is power and purposeful activity, which means intelligence and a purposive being. The universe cannot be the result of chance or blind force or chemical action and interaction. This universe did not cause itself. No other answer to what would otherwise be an unsolvable riddle can be found than that in the first verse of the first chapter of the Book of Beginnings, "In the beginning God" (Gen. 1:1).

In systematic theology this appeal to order in the universe is called the cosmological argument for the existence of God, or the argument from the cause of the cosmos or universe.

Design and orderly purpose witness to Him. We see everything in the world moving in orderly fashion. God was not only in the beginning its Creator, but his hand continues to be seen. The mountains still stand, the valleys are not filled up, rivers still run to the sea. The heavens have not fallen; there is still blue in the sky and warmth in the sun. The sun still comes up every morning at its appointed time, never a split second late. Season still follows season with resistless regularity. "Surely God is in this place," and we proclaim it, for "the heavens declare the glory of God" (Ps. 19:1).

Concerning God and His Revelation of Himself

Jesus made large use of this revelation of God in nature, seeing him in the "lilies of the field" and in everything, everywhere.

Spiritual ideals and values witness to Him. In spite of the evil and hate in the world, these are not ultimate. Sometimes it seems the world is in moral and spiritual chaos. But the laws operating in the moral and spiritual realm are as immutable and dependable as are those which operate in the material universe. "Whatsoever a man soweth, that shall he also reap" is even truer in morals than it is in agriculture.

Holiness or right is still stronger than sin or wrong. Truth will outlive error. Goodness will triumph over evil. Love will be marching on and winning long after the forces of hate have spent themselves and gone back to the pit whence they came.

God will save if you will have it so, but the same God will bring judgment on hate and every evil passion. Put more simply, this means that we have a witness to God in these values and forces, moral and spiritual, and we cannot see them operate without proclaiming that "God is."

History witnesses to Him. God's work in the world of men gives testimony to the fact that he is. History is the story of his work with man. The Bible is a special part of that history. But it is not all the story, for all history is *His* story. God is and always has been at work in the human process and is working out his purpose in the race which he created. This does not mean that all that has happened has been according to his will, but that he has made even that which is contrary to his purpose somehow work toward his ultimate purpose. God may be thwarted but he cannot ultimately be defeated.

Sometimes within the stream of human life and history, and sometimes seeming to cut across the stream, but always in the stream, God is at work. History is the record of a struggle, but God is in the struggle, and he is always fighting on the side of right, and in the end he will win.

Our fellow men witness to Him. History is simply the lengthened shadow of men. God has always worked with men, and the record of that work is history. God works in the lives of men today, changing, transforming, lifting life, giving it direction and meaning, and as fast as this happens it becomes history.

Your own life witnesses to Him. Your intelligence, your judgment, your will, your emotions, your conscience, your moral and spiritual nature, all witness to Him. And more than all that, you may know him by faith in personal experience. Your whole being longs for God; your heart hungers for him; your spirit thirsts for him; your soul pants for him as the hart pants for the water brook. You can find him, and when you find him you will know him and never let him go.

Jesus Christ supremely witnesses to Him. Jesus came into the world to reveal God to us even as he said, "He that hath seen me hath seen the Father" (John 14:9). "God with us" (Matt. 1:23), the angel said his name would be. "God was manifest in the flesh" (I Tim. 3:16), declared the great Apostle. Jesus is the supreme manifestation of God in human history. He was God's "deed," God's "act," in time and history. Except for the fact of God, Jesus is the world's unaccountable man.

The writer of the letter to the Hebrew Christians makes this most clear, and Goodspeed in his translation has made it most emphatic: "It was little by little and in different ways that God spoke in old times to our forefathers through the prophets, but in these latter days he has spoken to us in a Son, whom he had destined to possess everything, and through whom he had made the world. He is the reflection of God's glory, and the representation of his being" (Heb. 1:1-3).

We cannot account for this matchless One except on the basis of God. This we most surely believe, and this we most urgently proclaim.

The Bible as the Record of God's Revelation

We have noted God's general revelation of himself to man in nature. The Bible is a record begun in the very dawn of human history as God manifested himself and his will in nature, in history, and to the minds and hearts of men, even by supernatural intervention in the lives and in the stream of history. This revelation reaches its climax in Jesus Christ. But back of his coming was a long series of events which forms the history of the chosen people of the Old Testament, following which is the record of events concerning the church, along with the story of Christ in the New Testament. All of this the Bible sets forth as being of supreme significance, and we accept the Bible, therefore, as "God's self-revelation par excellence."

Concerning this record of God's revelation of himself, there are a number of points that you may want to consider in passing.

Revelation is progressive. God has revealed himself as man has been prepared to receive His revelations. That man knows so little about God, even today, is due not to any limitations in God but in man. The Old Testament shows us God preparing Israel as his servant and advancing His own purpose in the face of every obstacle until its triumphant culmination is reached in Jesus Christ.

Again it must be emphasized that Christ stands at the center of this unveiling of God. When we put Christ at the center, the meaning of the Bible becomes clear. Thus we read the Bible as a record of God's workings, each stage of the process determined not by the character of God, which is always the same, but by the capacity of man's mind to understand the character of God.

The Bible was written by inspiration. Revelation is God's impartation of the truth concerning himself; illumination is the divine quickening of man's being, so as to enable him to apprehend the truth which God revealed; inspiration is the quickening of man's functions, enabling him to communicate this truth.

We speak of the Bible as being the "inspired" Word of God; so speaks the Bible itself. As we read these inspired writings, God gives illumination to our minds, and we comprehend, and the knowledge of God comes to us; hence the Bible is a revelation of God to mankind. "All scripture is given by inspiration of God" (II Tim. 3:16).

To link inspiration with revelation and illumination, we must quote the rest of Paul's statement: "And is profitable for doctrine, for correction, for instruction in righteousness: that the man of God may be perfect, thoroughly furnished unto all good works." Inspiration, in the Greek, literally means "God-breathed." Man, "inbreathed" by the Divine Spirit, wrote what God had revealed, even as "holy men of God spake as they were moved by the Holy Ghost" (II Pet. 1:21).

Concerning God and His Revelation of Himself 15

In the Bible there comes to us a revelation which makes the Bible a unique book; it is the only one of its kind; there is none other like it. It brings to us a revelation of God like that which God gave to Paul: "By revelation he made known unto me the mystery . . . which in other ages was not made known unto the sons of man, as it is now revealed unto his holy apostles and prophets by the Spirit" (Eph. 3:3-5). This "mystery" is made clear in "the holy scriptures, which are able to make thee wise unto salvation through faith which is in Christ Jesus" (II Tim. 3:15).

Thus we take the Bible "not as the word of men, but as it is in truth, the word of God" (I Thess. 2:13); and thus we boldly proclaim that "man shall not live by bread alone, but by every word which proceedeth out of the mouth of God" (Matt. 4:4).

In and through the Bible we find God. In and through the Bible we find ourselves. It brings us face to face with the truth as it is in Jesus. The scope of the Bible's authority exactly coincides with the scope of the Bible's purpose, which is the redemption of man.

What Is God Like?

We approach the answer to this question "What is God like?" recognizing the limitations of human knowledge and the difficulty of discussing the Divine Being in terms of human words and human thought. The recognition of these limitations should deter us from dogmatism, and yet it should not keep us from affirming and proclaiming what we believe. "The secret things belong unto the Lord our God; but those things which are revealed belong unto us and to our children forever" (Deut. 29:29). And the things which belong to us, we positively affirm and boldly declare.

Defining God

Since God is limitless it is evident that there can be no full definition of him. Yet we can put into words our limited knowledge of him, and try to say what both our head and our heart tell us is true. We can make great affirmations and great declarations upon the basis of God's revelations of himself in his self-disclosures to man.

The word *God* means different things to different people, but we are here concerned with the Christian concept of God based upon what the Bible says about him.

Christian thinkers have phrased definitions such as this: "There is but one living and true God, who is a Spirit, everlasting, of infinite power, wisdom and goodness; the maker and preserver of all things, both visible and invisible. In this unity of the Godhead there are three persons, of one substance, power, and authority, the Father, the Son and the Holy Ghost." The so-called Apostle's Creed puts it, "I believe in God, the Father Almighty, Maker of heaven and earth." The Christian faith is that there is an infinite Person whom men ought to worship, who holds such relations to men that He is best described as Father; who is beyond the world and yet within it; and who reveals himself in nature, in the experiences of men, and supremely in Jesus Christ. Most definitions are too formal and cold to satisfy the Christian who wants to proclaim Him to others in some such declaration as "God is the loving heavenly Father whom Jesus revealed and of whom he taught"; or even more simply, "God is our Father."

Concerning God and His Revelation of Himself 17

The Attributes of God

By the attributes of God we mean those characteristics which we ascribe to him to indicate what he is in the essence of his being as he has revealed himself to men. Essence is precisely what a thing or person is. We cannot say what God is in the very essence of his Being, except in terms of unity, trinity, spirit, etc. But God has made known many of his characteristics in his dealings with man and in his messages to mankind. No effort at comprehensiveness will be made here.

God is one. He is a single and unitary being—the only one of his kind; he is one in the wholeness and harmony of his being. "The Lord he is God; there is none else beside him" (Deut. 4:35). "There is one God" (I Tim. 2:5). To a world of gods many and lords many, we want to cry, "Hear, O World, 'The Lord our God is one Lord; and thou shalt love the Lord thy God with all thine heart, and with all thy soul, and with all thy might'" (Deut. 6:4-5).

God is a personal Spirit. "God is a Spirit" (John 4:24). He is "the Father of spirits" (Heb. 12:9). By this we understand at least that he is not a material being. By personal we mean a being capable of self-consciousness and self-decision, or a being who is capable of functioning intelligently, emotionally, and volitionally—a being who thinks, feels, and wills. Personality does not necessarily involve physical being, therefore, we speak of God as a personal Spirit.

God is eternal. God is the eternally self-existent one. God is not a being of time, hence we speak of him as infinite, as over against man who is a time creature, or finite. He is the "high and lofty One that inhabiteth eternity" (Isa. 57:15), and we proclaim, "From everlasting to everlasting, thou are God" (Ps. 90:2).

God is invisible. "No man hath seen God at any time" (John 1:18). Of course he was manifested in Jesus as this same verse goes on to say.

God is almighty. Another way of saying this is to say he is omnipotent, or all-powerful. "I am the almighty God" (Gen. 17:1). "The Lord God omnipotent reigneth" (Rev. 19:6). "With God all things are possible" (Matt. 19:26). "There is nothing too hard for thee" (Jer. 32:17).

God can do all things that are the objects of power. His power is always a personal power, not blind force. He can do all that he needs to do for the accomplishment of his purpose which is sovereign and spiritual. He can do all things that are in harmony with the law of his being—all that his love and wisdom call him to do.

God is omniscient. He knows all and sees all. Nothing is hidden from him. "Great is our Lord, and of great power; his understanding is infinite" (Ps. 147:5). "Your Father knoweth" is the way Jesus stated it. "Neither is there any creature that is not manifest in his sight; but all things are naked and opened unto the eyes of him with whom we have to do" (Heb. 4:13).

God is omnipresent. We believe that space is no hindrance to God, for God is Spirit, everywhere present to know and to do according to his will. I can never be beyond his reach. "I only know I cannot drift beyond his love and care," for he has promised, "Lo, I am with you alway." We can rest on that. That we can proclaim. We can and must tell men that they cannot escape God. "Whither shall I go from thy spirit? or whither shall I flee from thy presence? If I ascend up into the heaven, thou art there; if I make my bed in hell, behold, thou art there. If I take the wings of the morning, and dwell in the uttermost parts of the sea; even there shall thy hand lead me, and thy right hand shall hold me" (Ps. 139: 7-10).

God is unchangeable. We sometimes say he is immutable. This does not mean that God is a static and not an active, dynamic Being, but that he is unchangeable in his nature, in his purposes, and motives for action. His power does not fluctuate. "I am the Lord, I change not" (Mal. 3: 6). He is "the Father of lights, with whom is no variableness, neither shadow of turning" (Jas. 1: 17).

He is not a being of moods or whims, nor is he subject to caprice. I can depend on him to act always in harmony with his nature, or character.

God is holy. He himself declares it, "I am holy" (Lev. 11: 44). Seraphim declare it: "Holy, holy, holy, is the Lord of hosts" (Isa. 6: 3). The emphasis of the whole Bible is upon the fact of the moral supremacy and moral majesty of God—the God of ineffable light and effulgent glory. He is a being of absolute moral perfection, just and perfect in all his ways. "God is light, and in him is no darkness at all" (I John 1: 5). Light is a symbol of purity.

God is just. "Just and right is he" (Deut. 32: 4). "Justice and judgment are the habitation of thy throne" (Ps. 89: 14). "Just and true are thy ways" (Rev. 15: 3). God is light and God is love, but also "our God is a consuming fire" (Heb. 12: 29). He will be absolutely fair to all. His judgments are never arbitrary, for sin brings its own judgment and its own condemnation.

God is merciful. This attribute of God is not set

over against justice, but is used to ascribe to God a love for the unworthy. If you want to read twenty-six statements of this fact of Divine revelation, read the endings of the twenty-six verses of Psalm 136.

It is this mercy which leads to forgiveness. "The Lord God, merciful and gracious, long-suffering, and abundant in goodness and truth, keeping mercy for thousands, forgiving iniquity and transgression and sin" (Exod. 34:6-7).

God is love. Love is the dynamic of God's being—of all his attributes. "God is love" (I John 4:8, 16). Love is God's abiding attitude toward men. It is God's essential nature to love. It is love's essential nature to give: "God so loved the world, that he gave his only begotten Son, that whosoever believeth in him should not perish, but have everlasting life" (John 3:16).

Was ever such love as that!

God is our Father. Could we conclude this section on what God is like better than by saying that he is "our Father"? This also is a summarization of all the moral characteristics of God. Holy love is the supreme characteristic of this Father.

This idea was not altogether foreign to Old Testament thought. Isaiah spoke of it in 63:16, "Doubtless thou art our Father." Malachi has a passage, "Have we not all one Father?" (2:10).

However, it remained for Jesus and the New Testament to give the idea full meaning. First of all God is "the Father of our Lord Jesus Christ" (Rom. 15:6). He is the "Father of light" (Jas. 1:17). He is the "Father of spirits" (Heb. 12:9). Most of all he is "our Father" who, "of his own will begat . . . us with the word of truth" (Jas. 1:18) through Christ, for "as many as received him, to them gave he power to become sons of God, even to them that believe on his name: which were born, not of blood, nor of the will of the flesh, nor of the will of man, but of God" (John 1: 12-13). This ties in with the attribute of love, for "behold what love the Father hath bestowed upon us, that we should be called the sons of God" (I John 3: 1). Therefore, "we cry, Abba, Father" (Rom. 8: 15).

God as Trinity

The doctrine of the Trinity, namely, that the Father, the Son, and the Holy Spirit are three persons of one essence is not merely the outcome of men's speculation. The doctrine grew out of the necessity of giving a rational explanation of the Christian experience of God in Christ through the working of the Holy Spirit.

Such Bible statements as the baptismal formula in Matthew 28: 19: "Baptizing them in the name of the Father, and of the Son, and of the Holy Ghost"; and the apostolic benediction in II Corinthians 13: 14: "The grace of the Lord Jesus Christ, and the love of God, and the communion of the Holy Ghost, be with you all," are one basis of the doctrinal concept of one God but three persons. Divine attributes ascribed to one are ascribed to the other persons of the Godhead.

The concept of God as a trinity came as a result of the activity of God and not as a baffling philosophical puzzle. It is not a mathematical formula but a religious one. The early Christians, with a background of belief in one God, came to experience and think of Jesus as God, for God made himself known to them in Jesus. Before Jesus went away he had promised to send the Holy Spirit. Then the Spirit came and the disciples experienced him as the indwelling personal presence of God.

So, as Christians, we are in fellowship with God in Christ, and we do the Father's will in the companionship of the Son and in the guidance and power of the Holy Spirit. This we believe, and this we proclaim.

THE WORKS OF GOD

We will here consider what we believe and what we proclaim concerning the mighty works of God our Father, including his creative activity, his providential work, both in nature and in history. His work in redemption will be reserved for another chapter.

In Creation

God not only is, but he is the cause and preserver of all that is. We are concerned with the creative work of God not only because the record of it is the only satisfactory account of the origin of things and of man but also because it helps us to understand the nature of God, gives spiritual insight into the universe in which we live and proclaims the proper relation between God and mankind. God's redemptive activity, as recorded in the Bible, was possible only on the basis of the fact that he created man.

When we say that God is the Creator we mean that "God is the maker of heaven and earth, and all that dwell therein." "In the beginning God created the heavens and the earth." (Gen. 1:1). "And God said, Let us make man in our image, after our likeness" (1:26). This shows God not only as the Primal Cause, but as the personal Creator of man as a person.

That God is Creator is the basis for the New Testament teaching concerning God's new creation. God is our Creator; herein is our hope. Something went wrong after God had made man in his own image. Came the fall. Came God's redemptive, re-creative activity. Now "if any man be in Christ, he is a new creature" (II Cor. 5:17). The divine image may be restored when we "put on the new man, which after God is created in righteousness and true holiness" (Eph. 4:24).

In Natural Providence

The concept of Divine Providence is not so much a doctrine as a way of thinking about God. It is our way of saying that the God who created pervades and sustains that which he created. It is our way of saying that the laws of nature are the laws of God. These laws are not the working of blind force but of personal power. "With all due allowance for the inherent forces in nature, yet it may be held in a very real sense that God clothes the grass of the field and feeds the fowls of the air. His directing agency permeates all his works" (Byrum, in *Christian Theology*). It is belief in the continuing activity of God which enables us to pray, "Give us this day our daily bread."

This we believe, and this we proclaim: This supreme God works through the ordinary processes of nature, and when necessary for the accomplishment of his purposes he works in extraordinary ways, which we call supernatural or miraculous. Whether natural or supernatural, it is all the working of God.

In History

It is the Christian faith that we serve a God who is able to make "all things work together for good to those who love God," to use the words of Paul's exultant affirmation.

God has a purpose for the race he created. His

purpose is redemptive. He will accomplish that purpose. He is now accomplishing it. In the end he will be victorious. He will accomplish it in spite of all that would hinder. God's purpose may be hindered, but it can never be defeated. God is at work to save the world, but if the world will not be saved, then he is at work to judge the world. History gives abundant proof of the reality of the moral order. And where in all history shall we look for sterner proof of this truth than in the life-and-death struggle that grips the nations today? The chaos, the tyranny, the despair, the folly of greed and war—surely our day should need no other or better proof of what happens when God is left out. It is a stern reminder that we live in a world where wrong will not work. For nation, for community, for individual, "the wages of sin is death."

Summary

God is the supreme giver of life. Upon him all the issues of life depend. He is not a problem to be solved but a Person to be loved and served. He is an object, not merely for discussion and debate, but for devotion.

All of this means that it is important to us what we believe about God. All this means that it is important to others what we proclaim about God.

Our faith is faith in a living God, in whom, and in whom alone, are hope, security, and salvation now and forever.

Our faith is in God, "the Father of our Lord Jesus Christ" and "our Father."

Possibly the highest thought we can have concerning God is that he is a Christlike God. For here we are affirming not merely theism, but Christian theism. Take any of the evidences of God's existence, any

Concerning God and His Revelation of Himself

analysis of his attributes, any listing of his works in creation and history, and think of them in the light of the nature, character, and works of Christ, and you will be helped to see God in his true meaning.

Can we not conclude this chapter with a declaration? This we believe, this we proclaim: God is *over* all—the Father whom we utterly trust, and to whom we give our lives in devotion; God is *through* all—through Jesus Christ supremely, and through everyone who opens his life to Him through Jesus; God is *in* all—the directing, empowering, sanctifying Spirit, making the Father and the Son real to us, reproducing in us the life of God, calling and sending us out to declare to all "the unsearchable riches" in that family of God which is his church; "one God and Father of all, who is over all and through all and in all."

Chapter II
CONCERNING MAN AND HIS PREDICAMENT

The Christian doctrine of man springs directly out of the Christian doctrine of God. The meaning of sin grew as the concept of God grew. In the light of the teaching of Jesus sin took on meanings quite different from its meanings under the Law, for instance. All the way through our study we shall be impressed with the relatedness and interrelatedness of all aspects of Christian doctrine. We need to know the truth about ourselves as well as about God.

This chapter deals with two rather distinct and yet closely related subjects, man and sin. It is man's sin, not sin in the abstract, with which we are dealing. Sin has been so determining a factor in the life of man that the nature of man cannot be studied apart from what sin has done to him.

"The proper study of mankind is man" said one of the great poets. It is not only the proper study, but it is one of the most difficult. "Know thyself" is a good dictum, but not an easy one to follow. "What is man?" is a question the psalmist asked long ago, but the full answer is not yet forthcoming. There are several branches of the general study of man, such as anthropology, physiology, psychology, and sociology. We can know some very definite things about man as a result of the first two disciplines; but in the other two which have to do with man's behavior, both as an individual and as a social being, we have much to learn. It is our purpose here to study man from the standpoint of religion, or theology, as a spiritual personality.

MAN AS HE WAS MADE

Here we must go to the Word of God. It alone holds the answer to questions about man's origin and destiny. The Bible is a record of God's education of man in the highest knowledge of what man himself is. It is a study of man in his relation to God.

His Origin

As a physical being man is "of the dust of the ground" by the hand of God; as a spiritual being he is by the breath of God. He is from both dust and Deity, and both these by the primary power and purpose of God. Man is a child of earth and a child of heaven. God is his creator. The doctrine of creation answers the questions, Whence came the universe? and Whence came man? It also interprets the universe and man in such a way as to provide a basis for answers to many other questions. God's creation of man is the first of a long list of events out of which come God's redemptive plan and the salvation which he gives.

That man is a created being is clearly taught in the Bible as a whole, not only in the first two chapters of Genesis. For in the Bible is a recital, not primarily of a philosophy concerning God, nor even of a doctrine of God, but of what God has done. And one of the things God has done is this: "God created man" (Gen. 1:27).

To fully appreciate the Genesis record of man's creation, the full account should be read in chapters 1:1— 3:24. Along with Genesis 1:26 look also at 2:7, both

Concerning Man and His Predicament

of which show that man was, at the time of his creation, a highly favored and exalted being. The whole ascending order of creation culminated in man, who was given dominion over all that had been created. But of more significance was the fact that man was in the divine image. More will be said about this in the next section of this chapter.

"Man" as used here means mankind, or the race—the whole species of human beings as descended from Adam. The race has a common origin. This means not only the biological unity of mankind, but the spiritual unity of mankind. This fact is involved in the Genesis command, "Be fruitful, and multiply, and replenish the earth," and in the woman's name, "Eve . . . the mother of all living" (3:20). Malachi's question (2:10), "Have we not all one father? hath not one God created us?" is echoed in Acts 17:26, "And hath made of one blood all nations of men . . . to dwell on all the face of the earth." All men of all the race are creatures of God—sons of God by creation and potential sons by a new creation.

His Constitution

Man's constitution is involved in his creation and in the creative process: the "dust of the ground" and "the breath of God" constituted man a "living soul" or being. On the basis of these facts man has been defined as "a spirit dwelling in a human body, but not entirely dependent upon it."

There is an outer or physical aspect of man's being, and there is an inner or spiritual aspect of it. "Twofold being" has been the term commonly used to express these two aspects of man's being. This twofoldness must not be construed in such a way that it negates man's essential unity of being or oneness of personality.

Man is a personal being. In studying the idea of God as a person, we defined "person" as a being self-conscious and self-determining—a being capable of functioning intelligently, emotionally, and volitionally—one who can think, feel, and will.

"The image of God" involves the concept of personality. It may, and does, involve more than that, but it at least involves that. This puts man in a different category from the merely animal creation. This we believe and this we proclaim, that man as a person is of infinite worth in God's sight and should be so regarded by every child of God.

Man is a physical being. We are not setting this idea over against, or as something apart from, the fact that man is a person; we are saying that this person, at least as presently constituted, is a physical being.

The Bible does not disparage the body as did Greek thought. Evidence of this is Jesus' concern for the bodily well-being of man. He spoke often of God's provision for and concern about food, clothing, and shelter. He even miraculously increased the loaves and fishes that men might be fed. He healed men of their physical ills and infirmities and continues to do so even to the present. He makes man's destiny in part dependent upon his concern for the physical well-being of his fellows, as is set forth in Matthew 25:35-44.

Paul put great emphasis upon the sacredness of the human body. "I beseech you therefore, brethren, by the mercies of God, that ye present your bodies a living sacrifice, holy, acceptable unto God" (Rom. 12:1). "What? know ye not that your body is the temple of the Holy Ghost, which is in you, which ye have of God, and ye are not your own? For ye are bought with a price: therefore, glorify God in your body, and in your spirit, which are God's" (I Cor. 6: 19-20).

The Christian concept of the human body adds much to the dignity and sacredness of human personality. It broadens the concept of Christian living, so that man may glorify God even in eating and drinking and all the ordinary activities of human life. The attitude toward the body can be either a holy one or a perverted one. And yet the body or physical aspect of man as a person is not the most essential element. "Fear not them which kill the body, but are not able to kill the soul" (Matt. 10:28). "Though our outward man perish, yet the inward man is renewed day by day" (II Cor. 4:16).

Man is a spiritual being. Man is a spirit dwelling in a body. Man is personal spirit, a spiritual as well as a material being.

In Genesis this spiritual nature is referred to as "the image of God." When "God breathed into his nostrils the breath of life . . . man became a living soul." Some would try to distinguish between spirit and soul, but it is a question whether the Bible will bear out such a distinction. Certainly such a distinction serves no practical purpose.

"The image of God" in which man was originally made means at least that he is a moral or spiritual personality—a being made in the likeness of God.

Man is related to God as creature to Creator. He is related to Him as servant is to master. He is also related to God as son to Father, even in creation. That metaphor takes on added meaning when through Christ man's sonship is made vitally spiritual.

This we believe, and this we proclaim to all men—they are all so constituted, in spite of sin, that they are potentially the sons of God. No one need despair.

Man As He Has Become

The Fall of Man

Genesis pictures man as a fallen being, as indeed does the entire revelation of God. His fall came as a result of disobedience. More will be said concerning this fact in a later portion of this chapter in a study of man's sin.

Adam's sin brought guilt and condemnation and separation from God. Separation from God is spiritual death. "The day that thou eatest thereof thou shalt surely die" (Gen. 2:17). "The wages of sin is death" (Rom. 6:23). Sin alienated man from God and from his fellows. Sin broke the communion between man and God.

Sin brought moral and spiritual unlikeness to God. Sin has continued to corrupt human nature ever since. This is true of sin as a racial quality and as personal transgression.

Man Is Corrupted by Sin

In the Bible we see both the abjectness and the grandeur of man. Created in the image of God—that is man's glory. Sinful, separated from God—that is man's shame.

This corruption of human nature has been called depravity, for man is depraved—though not totally. It is sometimes spoken of as "inborn" sin. However much difference of opinion there may be about the extent of it or about how it came to be or about how to be free from it, the fact of sin's existence is self-

Concerning Man and His Predicament 33

evident. It is written large in the Bible and in all history; it is also written large in the present scene.

Perhaps this corruption has been most correctly analyzed as a perversion of the entire personality of man—a derangement of the moral nature, whereby the judgment is clouded, the emotions are perverted, and the will is weakened, so that there is a tendency, urge, drive, or bent to the wrong instead of to the right.

Experience as recorded in the Bible indicates the universality of sin. It began with Adam, and it has continued in the race, much as Paul sets forth in Romans 1:21: "Because that, when they knew God, they glorified him not as God, neither were thankful; but became vain in their imaginations, and their foolish heart was darkened." David lamented, "I was shapen in iniquity, and in sin did my mother conceive me" (Ps. 51:5). Jeremiah observed, "The heart is deceitful above all things, and desperately wicked" (17:-9). Paul writes, "We all . . . were by nature the children of wrath, even as others" (Eph. 2:3). He gives his testimony, "I know that in me, (that is, in my flesh) dwelleth no good thing: for to will is present with me; but how to perform that which is good I find not. For the good that I would I do not: but the evil which I would not, that I do" (Rom. 7:18-19). Jesus states most emphatically, "Out of the heart . . . proceed evil thoughts" (Mark 7:21), and then goes on to give a long list of sins that come from the evil heart.

Though Jesus saw the moral corruption of man he saw also his spiritual possibilities. Zaccheus, in Luke 19:1-10, is seen as "a sinner" and at the same time as a "son of Abraham." For man, though in sin, is still a creature with something of the divine image implanted within, which all the depraving, defiling, and devastating effects of sin have not been able to destroy.

Man as a Sinner

Not only is the race in moral slavery, but sin is actual in each individual life that has come to the point of moral responsibility.

Sin is lawlessness. "Whosoever committeth sin transgresseth also the law, for sin is the transgression of the law" (I John 3:4). Sin is a transgression of the highest laws of human life, of the law of the moral universe, of the law of God himself, whether that law be expressed in the prohibitions of the Mosaic code, or in the "law of love" as laid down and exemplified by Jesus. It is transgression of that moral law of God by which the moral universe is governed. It is the violation of that law of God which is his rule for the lives of men. It is that law of which the psalmist wrote, "The law of the Lord is perfect, converting the soul: the testimony of the Lord is sure, making wise the simple" (Ps. 19:7). Any departure from, or lack of conformity to, that law is sin. It is a law written both in the Book and in the moral judgment of mankind. "For as many as have sinned without law shall also perish without law; and as many as have sinned in the law shall be judged by the law. . . . For when the Gentiles, which have not the law, do by nature the things contained in the law, these, having not the law, are a law unto themselves: which show the work of the law written in their hearts, their conscience also bearing witness, and their thoughts the meanwhile accusing or else excusing one another" (Rom. 2:12, 14-15).

Man, unregenerate, refuses to be governed by God, and seeks his own way according to his nature. Man

Concerning Man and His Predicament

rejects God's way and goes his own selfish way. "All we like sheep have gone astray; we have turned every one to his own way" (Isa. 53:6).

Sin is "missing the mark." Sin has been defined as "any violation of, or want of conformity to, the will of God." It is not only a positive doing of the wrong, but also a not doing of that which is right. "For all have sinned, and come short of the glory of God" (Rom. 3:23). It is coming short, not only of the glory of God, but of life's purpose. It is defeating God's purpose for our life. It is to "fall short of the high calling."

Sin is giving life over to unworthy purposes or things. Sin is any failure to choose the best—failure to live righteously or to act from highest motives. It is taking a lesser good when a greater is possible.

Sin is in attitude as well as in act. Sin is in every attitude and action which are out of harmony with the will of our heavenly Father. It is not only in acts such as murder and adultery, for John says, "Whosoever hateth his brother is a murderer" (I John 2:15), and Jesus declared, "Whosoever looketh on a woman to lust after her hath committed adultery with her already in his heart" (Matt. 5:28), but also in sins of attitude and disposition—envy and jealousy, which lead to hate, peevishness and sullenness, prejudice and injustice, unkindness and oppression. How great in number and variety are such sins!

Not doing one's duty is sin. "To him that knoweth to do good, and doeth it not, to him it is sin" (Jas. 4:17). If one, like the priest and the Levite, sees the hurt of the world and "passes by on the other side," is not that sin? If one wraps his pound in a napkin and does not use it, is that not sin?

Failure to believe in God through Jesus Christ is sin. See John 3:18. And if loving God with the whole heart, soul, mind, and strength, and one's neighbors as himself are the greatest commandments, would not the failure to do this be the greatest sin? Broken sonship, refusal of love and obedience to an all-wise and all-loving Father, is sin.

From all the foregoing, it is plain to see that sin is factual, and it is actual, and it is awful. Keep in mind that we are here considering man and his sin.

But there is another side to this picture of what man is, and what can be done about his sin.

Man Still a Person

Man is not utterly ruined, even though he is badly wounded. Man was made righteous, with capacity for free communion with God and with grace to enable him to enjoy that communion. By his own choice he lost that capacity and the grace which went with it. Yet his reason was not totally perverted, his will not entirely depraved, his desires not directed solely and wholly toward evil. There is an undergirding from God, a continuing modicum of grace, which causes him to "hunger and thirst after righteousness" and to pant for God—which makes him able to respond by God's grace to the good which he desires. Man is in a dilemma, but there is a way out.

In sending his Son into the world to save man it is evident that God placed great value upon man. Our day is characterized by a developing pessimism, even a thoroughgoing cynicism, about man. Man as a person may be in the grip of sin, but man as a person can be changed and lifted out of and above sin. He can be saved from sin, and the divine image can be restored.

Concerning Man and His Predicament

More must be said about this in another chapter but this much needs to be said right here.

In saying that man is a person, we mean more than that he is a being with eyes that look out and up and a body that walks erect. We mean more than that he is a being with the power of reason, who can form general ideas and interpret what his senses bring, and so enlarge his ideas and have dominion in the world. We mean more than that he has the ability to use speech for the transmission of ideas. Saying these things we are saying much, but in saying that he is a person we are saying more than all these put together.

By "person" we mean to convey the idea that man is a being with the power of self-conscious decision, a being with intelligence, emotions, and will.

In making man, God made him a person, in the image of himself, a being with the power of self-grasp, self-estimation, and self-determination. The power of self-estimation is the power to say I AM—I am a self, a person; I am I—not another; it is the power to say *I know, I feel, I will.*

Man is a moral person under moral demand. This is written into the very constitution of man's being. The "image of God" is a moral and spiritual nature. "There is a spirit in man." This is brought out in the New Testament, where the image of God is represented as being restored in regeneration. "Put on the new man, which after God is created in righteousness and true holiness" (Eph. 4:24). "And have put on the new man, which is renewed in knowledge after the image of him who created him" (Col. 3:10).

Man is under moral demand. He is under demand

of the law of God, which is holy, as previously shown in the quotation from Romans 2:12-15.

Man is a being with a conscience. This fact has its basis in man's constitution as a person with the moral law written into his very nature. If man can use his mind to form judgments concerning right and wrong; if he feels a compulsion to do the right and to avoid the wrong; if he can choose the right and reject the wrong—all of which is the function of personality—then he has what we call a conscience.

Conscience may be said to be "the functioning of a person in the realm of morals." It is the forming of moral judgments. By the use of his mind, man may know right and wrong. He does not instinctively know this, but he can by a study of life and especially by the revelation of God in the Bible come to know what is right and what is wrong. Then on the basis of what he believes to be right or wrong as the case may be, he does feel that he "ought" to do the right and "ought not" to do the wrong. By the use of his power to will or decide, he acts. His conscience approves if he does the right and disapproves if he does the wrong.

Man Is a Free Being

The very idea of personality involves the idea of freedom, or the power of choice. Of course man is not free in the absolute sense. But he does have power within limits to make free choices. Man is responsively free. And responsibility involves ability to respond. Unless a choice is freely made it does not have moral quality.

As I wrote a number of years ago in *Toward Understanding God:* "Any theology, any philosophy, any moral science, any psychology, any sociology, which holds that man's choices are determined or compelled by forces outside of himself—himself, a being capable of self-conscious decision—is to be rejected; and it does not matter whether that force which compels choice be the 'will of God' in a theological formula; or 'the fates' in philosophy; or physical mechanism as in some forms of behavioristic psychology; or the 'environmental factors' in sociology."

Sometimes that margin of freedom of choice and action may be narrow, but it is there or man cannot be held spiritually accountable for his choices and conduct.

Enhancing this inherent power of choice in human personality, the grace of God comes to the aid of man and enables him to choose the right. The power of God is greater than all mechanistic powers—for spiritual powers are the greatest in the world—and it endows the believer with a more-than-human power which strengthens the will and makes him more than conqueror. Man has freedom of choice, but in order to exercise that freedom in the highest spiritual action, he needs the spiritual dynamic of the grace of God. This God has promised. This God gives. This freedom and power come through Christ as stated in such passages as John 8: 32-36: "And ye shall know the truth and the truth shall make you free. They answered him, We be Abraham's seed, and were never in bondage to any man: how sayest thou, Ye shall be made free? Jesus answered them, Verily, verily, I say unto you, whosoever committeth sin is the servant of sin. And the servant abideth not in the house forever: but the Son abideth ever. If the Son therefore shall make you free, ye shall be free indeed."

Consequences of Sin

The symbol of the serpent, first and fitting emblem of sin, shows its true nature. Sin brings poison into life, and death to all who feel its fangs. "The wages of sin is death" (Rom. 6:23). Death means separation from God. "Your iniquities have separated between you and your God, and your sins have hid his face from you" (Isa. 59:2). "When lust hath conceived it bringeth forth sin; and sin, when it is finished, bringeth forth death" (Jas. 1:15). Sin means death here and now; it means also eternal death: "Ye . . . shall die in your sins; whither I go, ye cannot come" (John 8:21).

Sin is not a fantasy; it is a fact. It has broken the relationships which man was created to sustain between man and God and between man and man. And it has brought conflict into the life of man himself. The destructive quality of sin is seen in the fact that man is lost—lost not only to God but to his highest self. Sin brings guilt—guilt before God—and this sense of guilt is always a disruptive and divisive factor in human life. Sin has soiled the purity of man's heart, killed the joy of his life, disturbed the peace of his conscience. It binds men in slavery. It brings personality conflicts, and creates many of the tensions and complexes which are so prevalent in human life and society today, for in sinning man sets himself over against the laws that really work, the only laws that will work, in the universe. In its very nature sin is a disorganizing principle which brings about a disintegration of life and personality. No one can ever build life harmoniously around a wrong principle, such as hate or pride or selfishness, for in their very nature all of these are disruptive and divisive, disintegrating and disorganizing. It is only

Concerning Man and His Predicament

when sin is taken out of life and God is put at the center that the inner life is made whole and that man is brought into harmony with God, his fellow man, and the moral forces which rule in the universe. More will be said on this point in the chapter on salvation.

AFFIRMATIONS OR SUMMING UP

Sin is inner moral wrongness and is as universal as is the race. Wrong conduct and acting from wrong motives are sin. Creation speaks of the dignity and spirituality of man, his responsible freedom, and his final destiny.

The greatest thing in the world is not the powers of nature or of mechanical operation, but the potentiality of spiritual personality.

The cross is the clue to man's worth.

Jesus recognized the value of all men—of any man—whether Nicodemus the Jew in Jerusalem, the Samaritan woman at Sychar, the Greek from Decapolis, the woman from Syrophoenecia, the despised publican, the blind beggar, the outcast woman, the demoniac, or the Pharisee—he saw each of them as a potential child of God.

Jesus was concerned not only about all men, but also about all of man and all that affected man.

Sin is inner moral wrongness, impurity at the very fountain of life, and it is as universal as is the race.

Sin is "lawlessness." This lawlessness manifests itself in many ways: toward God as unbelief, toward others as selfishness, toward self as pride.

Man is a son of God by creation. That sonship has been broken by sin. It may be restored in Christ. Man's real nature is to be found, not in what he is, but in what he may become.

Chapter III

CONCERNING CHRIST AND HIS REDEMPTIVE WORK

We have studied about God. We have studied about man and the severing of his proper relationship to God.

This infinite and holy God has taken action in behalf of finite and sinful man by sending his Son into the world. This Son of God and Son of man has entered uniquely and decisively into human history for the purpose of accomplishing the redemption of the sinful human race.

In Jesus Christ God has not only revealed himself but has poured into the stream of human life a new stream of Divine life. In Jesus Christ is a life-giving power. Christ himself is that power, and to as many as receive him, to them he gives "power to become the sons of God" (John 1:12). He gave himself on the cross, letting loose power for the changing of human life, taking away sin, and bringing man back into right relation with God and with his fellows. God still gives himself, his life, his power, his love, to raise man to the plane of sonship.

This is not merely history; it is the continuing and present experience of those who believe.

Christ is the central fact, the supreme Person, of the Christian Way. It is Christ whose name we bear, whose teaching we believe, whose life we share, and whose message we proclaim. It is Christ whom we follow and obey. It is Christ whose cause we serve by sharing with him in his work to save lost men. He is the One through whom God comes to man and through whom man comes to God.

The study in this chapter will be based on the truth contained and involved in such Scripture passages as the following: "There is one God, and one mediator between God and men, the man Christ Jesus" (I Tim. 2:5). "God, who at sundry times and in divers manners spake in time past unto the fathers by the prophets, hath in these last days spoken unto us by his Son, whom he hath appointed heir of all things, by whom also he made the worlds; who being the brightness of his glory, and the express image of his person, and upholding all things by the word of his power, when he had by himself purged our sins, sat down on the right hand of the Majesty on high" (Heb. 1:1-3). "God so loved the world that he gave his only begotten Son that whosoever believeth on him should not perish but have everlasting life" (John 3:16).

The study will be built around three main centers of reference: (1) Christ's Mission of Redemption; (2) Redemption by Reconciliation; and (3) Son of God and Son of Man.

CHRIST'S MISSION OF REDEMPTION

However we look at it, or whatever terms may be used to express it, Christ's purpose and work are redemptive.

In the next chapter we shall deal with the work of salvation, which in meaning is almost synonymous with redemption. But we shall for our purpose here use "redemption" as referring to the part which Christ plays in the saving process by atoning for man's sins,

Concerning Christ and His Redemptive Work

and "salvation" as referring to what Christ does in the hearts and lives of men by forgiving them, cleansing them, filling them with his presence, and so on.

Redeemer and Redemption

"Redeemer" is a name used for both the Father and the Son over and over again in the Scriptures. "To redeem" is a verb found many times. "Redemption" is frequently found in the Bible and in all works of theology. It sums up God's work in behalf of men.

Redemption in the Old Testament. In Leviticus 25:47-52 the medium of "redemption" is money paid for the recovery of a man's freedom. The consecration of the Levites to God redeems the first born (Num. 3:45-46). The word is frequently used in reference to the release of men and women from slavery (Exod. 6:6; Lev. 25:-47-48). And it is many times used in association with great national deliverances such as from Egyptian slavery and the Babylonian Captivity.

Even in the Old Testament the word is used to set forth deliverance from sin and return to God. Isaiah declares in a striking way that God is the Redeemer of his people from sin (59:20). See also Psalm 130:8.

Redemption in the New Testament. Here the teaching is not only extensive but deep and rich. The price paid is Christ's blood as in Acts 20:28 and I Peter 1:18-19. Redemption is by Christ's sacrificial death and from sin by grace (Eph. 1:7; Heb. 9:15). It is final and complete deliverance from every effect of sin, even death itself (Luke 21:28; Rom. 8:19-23; I Cor. 15:24-26).

Christianity is a religion of redemption. Religions may be thought of as religions of nature, of law, or of redemption. Christianity is a religion of redemption, for it sees man as needing something beyond what nature provides and something more than law to bring knowledge of what God requires. By nature man is enmeshed in sin and is lost, and law is powerless so far as bringing deliverance goes. Man cannot save himself. Since man cannot reach up to God, God must reach down to men. This he has done in Jesus Christ, his Son.

Christ's Work Is Redemptive Work

All that Jesus did and does is redemptive, but the focus of his redemption is in the power of love revealed on the cross, and the power of life as revealed in his resurrection. All that he is now doing as mediator flows from his death and resurrection.

Jesus regarded his mission as saving. It was clearly in the consciousness of Jesus that his mission was a saving mission—he came to save man. His gracious and glorious declaration in Luke 19:10 is the key to his purpose in coming into the world: "For the Son of man is come to seek and to save that which was lost."

There may be many ways of saying what the mission of Jesus was, but any way you say it, it turns out to be redemptive. If we say he came to set up his kingdom, that kingdom turns out to be redemptive, and the citizens of that kingdom are all who are redeemed by his blood, and it is entered only by a new birth. If we say it is to build his church, that church is "the church of God which he hath purchased with his own blood" (Acts 20:28).

In redeeming He humbled himself. What a sweeping statement is that in Philippians 2:6-11: "Who, being in the form of God, thought it not robbery to be equal with God; but made himself of no reputation, and took upon him the form of a servant, and was made in the likeness of men: and being found in fashion as a man, he humbled himself and became obedient unto death, even the death of the cross. Wherefore God also hath highly exalted him, and given him a name which is above every name: that at the name of Jesus every knee should bow . . . and . . . every tongue should confess that Jesus Christ is Lord, to the glory of God the Father."

In His mission he laid down his life. This he did both on behalf of men as his brethren and of God his Father. "I am the good shepherd: the good shepherd giveth his life for the sheep"; "I am the good shepherd, and know my sheep, and am known of mine. As the Father knoweth me, even so know I the Father: and I lay down my life for the sheep" (John 10:11, 14-15). "Greater love hath no man than this, that a man lay down his life for his friends" (15:13), but "God commendeth his love toward us, in that, while we were yet sinners, Christ died for us" (Rom. 5:8). "The Son of man came not to be ministered unto, but to minister, and to give his life a ransom for many" (Mark 10:45).

Thus we see that our Lord regarded himself as on a mission of redemption. This redemption could be accomplished only by Christ's leaving his home in glory and coming in the body of his humiliation—by the self-sacrifice of himself on the cross.

This is the gospel—the good news. This is what we believe. This is what we proclaim.

REDEMPTION BY RECONCILIATION

The Good News in Christ

"God was in Christ, reconciling the world to himself" (II Cor. 5:19). This also we believe and this also we proclaim—because it is the only way for ourselves and for the world. We have this assertion on no less authority than that of Paul, the greatest proclaimer of the gospel that the world has ever known: "All things are of God, who hath reconciled us to himself by Jesus Christ, and hath given us the ministry of reconciliation; to wit, that God was in Christ, reconciling the world unto himself, not imputing their trespasses unto them; and hath committed unto us the ministry of reconciliation. Now then we are ambassadors of Christ, as though God did beseech you by us: we pray you in Christ's stead, be ye reconciled to God" (5:18-20).

The quotation has been given at length, for within the compass of this passage Paul has set forth fully just what the good news is and what we are to do about that good news.

The theological term for this truth is the "doctrine of the atonement." However, the Scripture term is "reconciliation." The word "atonement" is used once in the New Testament (Rom. 5:11): "Jesus Christ, by whom we have now received the atonement." The word "atonement" is rendered "reconciliation" in the margin, and is so translated in the American Standard Version and the Revised Standard Version. It is so translated in verse 10. Whichever word is used, the central idea is that by Christ men are reconciled, made "at-one," with God.

The need of all men is to "be . . . reconciled to God" (II Cor. 5:20). The deed of the one God revealed is: "God was in Christ, reconciling the world unto himself" (5:19). The fact of history is that "we were reconciled to God by the death of his Son" (Rom. 5:10). The experience of the Christian is described:

Concerning Christ and His Redemptive Work 49

"Being justified by faith, we have peace with God through our Lord Jesus Christ" (Rom. 5:1). The work of the Christian is declared: "We pray you in Christ's stead, be ye reconciled to God" (II Cor. 5:20).

Theories of Atonement

During the Christian Era men have worked out many theories, setting forth in theological or philosophical terms the meaning of reconciliation or atonement. It is but natural that such should be done, but we are here dealing not with a theory but with the great fact of the Scripture and of Christian experience, namely that "God was in Christ reconciling the world unto himself." This is something God did. Atonement or reconciliation is God's deed; it is God acting in human life and human history. The incarnation, the life, the death, and the resurrection of Jesus Christ are all events that stand or fall together, and reconciliation is the result of these great facts.

However, it is well to understand some of the more prevalent theories which have been proposed as answers to the question: How does God save man? What part does the death of Christ play in God's work of redemption? However, keep in mind that the death of Christ and its efficacy is of such tremendous meaning that no theory, nor all of them put together, can adequately explain the fact. It is not an understanding of any or all theories of the atonement that saves man—it is faith in God through the merits and power of that great deed of God. The full truth of the atonement is too big to be tucked away neatly in any simple theory.

In looking at these theories we may remind ourselves that each of them at most can express but one or two aspects of the total meaning. At best no one of them can reflect more than certain elements of the total truth.

The main theories fall in the following categories as set forth in *The Wondrous Cross* by the author of this present writing:

"1. Those centering around the idea of sacrifice, with the sacrifice of an animal or bird as the symbol of that idea.

"2. Those growing out of the idea of ransom, as that of a slave, with the crudest form being that Christ's death was a ransom price paid to Satan.

"3. Those involving government or law court procedures, which are forensic in their nature, and represent Jesus as our substitute, taking our place, or even paying the penalty for our sin. This theory has strikingly stated that Jesus, in those few hours on the cross, suffered as much as all the souls of men would have suffered in an eternal hell.

"4. Those centering around such terms as 'satisfaction,' 'expiation,' and 'propitiation,' which represent God as propitiated because the price has been paid and justice has been satisfied.

"5. Those centering around the idea that the value of Jesus' death is in the influence of a good man who died rather than do evil, who loved truth and right enough to die for them. This example influences man to love God.

"6. Those centering around the idea of Christ's death being revelatory, expressing God's love and holiness and judgment of sin."

Doubtless, there is some element of truth in each of these attempts to explain the significance of Christ's death. But whether we think of it in terms of sacrifice,

Concerning Christ and His Redemptive Work 51

ransom, substitution, propitiation, governmental atonement, satisfaction, moral influence, or revelation, the fact is that God himself was the one who provided the sacrifice, paid the ransom, or made the propitiation. And a further fact is that it was for the purpose of reconciling man to God, for "God was in Christ reconciling the world to himself."

Whatever truth each of these theories contains grows out of the fact that reconciliation is the work of a personal God for men, who are persons. Quoting again from *The Wondrous Cross:*

"Possibly the one theory which comes nearest to stating a philosophy of the atonement, and which can be so stated as to include the truth of other theories is to be found in the 'revelatory' theory. It seems to come nearest to expressing what the death of Christ was to accomplish. The cross was God's way of redeeming men, and out of its revelational value comes its redemptive value. The cross becomes the means of a personal relevation of a personal God in the person of his Son, to persons. This explanation puts the emphasis upon the personal, as over against the impersonal values of some of the other theories. This says most emphatically that redemption is personal, that Christ's death is a redemptive power made operative in human life through this expression of divine love and divine judgment, and that it is redemptively creative in that it makes personal that mystical union of God with the believer in such a way that Christ's poured-out life may be poured in, or imparted to, the believer. God redeems man by revealing his love and, paradoxical though it may be, reveals his love by redeeming."

Having said this, let us again say that atonement or redemption or reconciliation is something which God did and does. The deepest meaning of the cross is that the highest law of life is the law of self-giving love, and this was fully demonstrated on the cross. We need to see the whole of what God does in terms of the personal, rather than in abstractions such as "moral influence," "governmental atonement," and so on.

The Fact of Atonement

In Christ God comes to man. In Christ man comes to God. God became man, that man might come to him. He gave his Son that we might become sons of God. Since man by his sin separated himself from God, and since sinful man could not reach up to God, God must come down to us. In Jesus Christ he has done just this. "For God so loved the world that he gave his only begotten Son that whosoever believeth on him should not perish but have everlasting life" (John 3:16). This is the very heart of the Christian faith, "For it pleased the Father that in him should all fullness dwell; and having made peace through the blood of his cross, by him to reconcile all things unto himself" (Col. 1:19-20).

Scripture could be piled text on text showing this fact. Many have already been cited, but here are a few more: "This is my blood of the new testament, which is shed for many for the remission of sins" (Matt. 26:28); "He hath made him to be sin for us, who knew no sin; that we might be made the righteousness of God in him" (II Cor. 5:21); "Christ hath redeemed us from the curse of the law, being made a curse for us" (Gal. 3:13); "Who his own self bare our sins in his own body on the tree, that we, being dead to sins, should live unto righteousness: by whose stripes ye were healed" (I Pet. 2:24); "Ye were not redeemed with corruptible things, as silver and gold . . . but with the precious blood of Christ, as of a lamb without blemish and without spot" (1:18-19).

With all this in mind, we can join the song of the eternally redeemed singing, "Thou art worthy . . . for thou wast slain, and hast redeemed us to God by thy blood" (Rev. 5:9). In Christ is atonement—in Christ is reconciliation, for in him and on his cross, "mercy and truth are met together; righteousness and peace have kissed each other" (Ps. 85:10).

SON OF GOD, SON OF MAN

To put some things into a simple statement is not easy, nor is it always easy to understand the simple statement after you have it. It is easy to say, "Jesus was a man." It is simple to say, "Jesus was God." They are not easy to understand when standing alone, but they become quite incomprehensible when they are put together, and we affirm that Jesus is Son of God and Son of man. "Great is the mystery of godliness; God was manifest in the flesh" (I Tim. 3:16).

And yet this the Bible affirms, and this we believe, and this we proclaim. It is one of those truths which may be to great for our minds but not for our hearts. Drink in the grandeur of it as you consider John 1:1-3, 14: "In the beginning was the Word, and the Word was with God, and the Word was God. The same was in the beginning with God. All things were made by him, and without him was not anything made that was made. . . . And the Word was made flesh, and dwelt among us (and we beheld his glory, the glory as of the only begotten of the Father), full of grace and truth."

The Word that was God and the Word that was flesh are not two realities to be set over against each other. Nor are they merely two separate facts to be set alongside each other. They belong together and are necessary even to begin to explain Jesus Christ our Savior. They are two facts of the unique Person. Possibly this should not seem strange to us, for after all, are God and man at his best very far apart except in finiteness and infinity? Man was created in "the image of God" and Christ came to the world as "the express image of his person" (Heb. 1:3). Christ must have been divine because he was so perfectly human, and how can we talk of his perfection of humanity except on the basis of Divinity? That "Word" which was "with God" and which "was God" became incarnate in Jesus Christ who was truly God and truly man.

Not for the purpose of separating them, but for analysis we will look at both aspects of this incarnation.

In Him We Know God

In Jesus we see and know God as living, loving, redeeming Person. In him we know God as Savior. "They shall call his name Emmanuel . . . God with us," and "Thou shalt call his name JESUS; for he shall save his people from their sins" (Matt. 1:23, 21).

"The Word was God" and "the Word became flesh" so that in Him is the greatest—the full and final—revelation of God.

In Him we know what God is like. We see God revealed in all his fullness, power, wisdom, holiness, and love. The attributes we ascribe to God the Father are made personal in Jesus the Son. All these ethical attributes of the Father about which we have already studied we see manifest in Jesus—expressing themselves in the life and work of Jesus. Otherwise, we would have to try to think of them as abstractions; but in Jesus they are concretely expressed. Love is seen in action; holiness is seen in his life; forgiving grace is seen on the cross; power is seen at work healing men, helping men, saving men.

We know God by what Jesus was. In his very nature he was like God. "He that hath seen me hath seen the Father" (John 14:9). "He that seeth me, seeth him that sent me" (12:45). "If ye had known me, ye should have known my Father also" (8:19). "I and my Father are one" (10:30). "And this is life eternal, that they might know thee the only true God, and Jesus Christ, whom thou has sent" (17:3). This is also brought out by what have been called the "I Am's" of Jesus:

"Before Abraham was, I am" (John 8:58).

"I am in the Father" (14:10).

"I am the living bread which came down from heaven" (6:51).

"I am the way, the truth, and the life" (14:6).

"I am the light of the world" (8:12).

"I am the true vine" (15:1).

"I am the resurrection and the life" (11:25).

"I am Alpha and Omega, the first and the last" (Rev. 1:11).

We know God by what Jesus said. His words are words of truth and they are words of authority. It were arrogance for anyone less than the Son of God to say, "Moses said unto you" thus and so, "but I say unto you" and then go on to give words to supersede the words of Moses as in Matthew 5:21-44.

"Never man spake like this man" (John 7:46).

"The words that I speak unto you, they are spirit, and they are life" (6:63).

"He taught them as one having authority, and not as the scribes" (Matt. 7:29).

We Know God by what others said of Jesus. Let us ask others concerning what they thought of Jesus.

Judas, you who betrayed him, what do you think of him? "I have betrayed . . . innocent blood" (Matt. 27:4). Pilate, you who tried to wash the blood from your hands, what do you say? "I find no fault in him." Centurion, you who helped drive the nails, what is your verdict? "Truly, this was the Son of God." Demons, you who know his power, do you have a word? "This was the Son of God." John, let us have your testimony. "Behold, the Lamb of God, which taketh away the sin of the world." Martha, do you want to witness? "Thou art the Christ, the Son of God." John, the apostle, you leaned on his breast, what is your well-considered verdict? "Jesus is the Christ, the Son of God." Peter, you who once denied him, whom do you say that he is? "Thou art the Christ, the Son of the living God." And Thomas you doubted—did you recover your faith? "My Lord and my God." Paul, you persecuted him and his followers; what is your final conclusion? "God was in Christ, reconciling the world to himself." Angels of heaven, what say you? "A Savior which is Christ the Lord." And God, Jesus' Father and ours, what dost thou declare? "This is my beloved Son, in whom I am well pleased, hear ye him."

In Jesus We Know Man

There is little point in affirming the deity of our Lord without also affirming his humanity. He was a man with all that that means. He was the race man. He was the "Son of man." That seems to have been the term which he most used in referring to himself.

He came to show us what God is and what man may be by the grace of God.

His humanity is not declared alone by his human

Concerning Christ and His Redemptive Work 57

birth and childhood during which he "grew in stature" but also by the fact that he grew "in wisdom, and in favor with God and man." He was "tempted in all points like as we are" and in all things save sin "was made like unto his brethren."

This Son of man and Son of God is our actual Redeemer. Both his divinity and his humanity are authenticated by great facts of our own life and time. There is still the fact of Jesus, the fact of the church, the fact of Christian experience; there is the further fact of nearly twenty centuries of homage; his words, "He that hath seen me, hath seen the Father" have proved true countless millions of times in the lives of "ten thousand times ten thousand, and thousands of thousands" of every age and clime.

Summary

It is just here in the area which we have been exploring that we find the eternal gospel, which we believe and which we proclaim. The "good news" is that Christ who lived, taught, died, rose again, and ever lives at the right hand of God has made provision for eternal redemption for all men; for "God was manifest in the flesh, justified in the Spirit, seen of angels, preached unto the Gentiles, believed on in the world, received up into glory" (I Tim. 3:16).

By his redemptive life and death Jesus had made possible the reconciliaton of sinful man to God. For God is reconciled to man, and in Jesus man may be reconciled to God. This is the gospel—"so we preach, and so ye believed" (I Cor. 15:11). This we believe—this we proclaim.

Redemption is something which God does in Jesus Christ. It is not something we do for ourselves. In Jesus we did not offer a sacrifice to God as a propitiation; it was God who offered the sacrifice—"the Lamb of God, which taketh away the sin of the world."

The cross is the clue to Christ's whole life, for his whole life was redemptive. His kingdom is a kingdom of the redeemed, and his church is at once the expression and organ of his redemptive purpose. Even with a clear vision of his redemptive purpose as pictured by that cross, we shall not be able to understand fully the "mystery of godliness." Without that cross we shall not be able to understand it at all.

He was the only begotten Son of God; all his life proceeded from the Father, was brooded over by the Father. "In him dwelleth all the fullness of the Godhead bodily" (Col. 2:9). All the love, the truth, the purpose, the holiness of God, came to fruition in this One. He was the Son of man—all the race was somehow caught up in the purpose of God in the full sweep of his redemptive love. And it is all done in Christ right here in our world.

Chapter IV

CONCERNING CHRISTIAN EXPERIENCE AND LIFE

We have glimpsed something of the nature and purpose of the Eternal Father in the sending of his Son for the redemption of the sinful race. Christ, who is salvation, "the way, the truth and the life," has made a new way to God.

Christ came as Savior: "Thou shalt call his name Jesus, for he shall save his people from their sins" (Matt. 1:21). A savior, if he really is one, saves. If Christ is to be our Savior he must do something for us. What is this he does for us? It is our purpose in this chapter to find out, at least in part.

Christ has provided redemption. Man must respond to that redemptive purpose of God in Christ.

Christian Experience

Christian experience is an experience of Christ and with Christ. It is being brought into right relation with God in and through Christ; it is being brought into right relation with one's fellow men; it is being brought into right relation inwardly—within the person himself.

We speak of this experience in many ways, using many figures of speech, and illustrate it in many ways. Some of these ways may state it more clearly than others, but all are needed if the full scope of what God has done, does, and will do for man is to be understood, even in part.

Christian Experience Is an Experience of Christ

First of all lay this down as a basic fact: Christ is life: "I am the way, the truth, and the life" (John 14:6). Then add to this the further basic fact: Christ came to give life: "I am come that they might have life, and that they might have it more abundantly" (10:10); "Because I live, ye shall live also" (14:19). This means not only a future life but also a present life, for "He that heareth my word, and believeth on him that sent me, hath everlasting life, and shall not come into condemnation, but is passed from death unto life" (5:24).

This life is a new kind of life—even eternal life—for "this is life eternal, that they might know thee, the only true God, and Jesus Christ whom thou hast sent" (17:3). This new life here is the guarantee of life beyond life, and leads to the fulfillment of life even in death. One who has this life can say with Paul, "O death, where is thy sting?" (I Cor. 15:55).

Let us therefore examine these facts and this experience of life in the light of the teaching of the Word which is "the word of life" (Phil. 2:16).

Christian experience comes through a new birth. This new birth comes by receiving Christ. "He came unto his own, and his own received him not. But as many as received him to them gave he power to become the sons of God, even to them that believe on his name: which were born, not of blood, nor of the will of the flesh, nor of the will of man, but of God" (John 1:11-13). This "receive him" means to receive him by faith, "even to them that believe on his name." More will be said about this in another connection in this chapter. For as we try to think through what God provides in this

Concerning Christian Experience and Life 61

experience, we need also to think of the conditions on which this experience may be had by man.

This concept of Christian experience as a new kind of life makes it easier to comprehend the declaration of Jesus to Nicodemus, "Except a man be born again, he cannot see the kingdom of God" (John 3:3). This new life is a new kind of life; it is the life of the Spirit, for "that which is born of the flesh is flesh; and that which is born of the Spirit is spirit" (vs. 6). This fact is indisputable. Jesus would say to us as to Nicodemus, "Marvel not that I said unto thee, Ye must be born again" (vs. 7). This is another of God's "musts"—a divine imperative.

The new birth is the beginning of a new kind of life. No one can be in right relation with God until he is "born again," which means "born from above." No one is in the "beloved community" or family of God, or kingdom of God, until he is born again.

This truth of the new birth is expressed also in the term "regeneration." Sinful man is dead in sin and must be made alive. It is also called a "new creation." "If any man be in Christ he is a new creature" (II Cor. 5:17). One translation gives this as "new creation." This is the fulfillment of a promise given through Ezekiel, "A new heart also will I give you, and a new spirit will I put within you" (36:26).

Christian experience is an experience of sonship. "To as many as received him to them gave he power to become sons of God" (John 1:12) is worthy of being proclaimed over and over again. This means that through Christ the "only begotten Son" we can become sons of God. "And because ye are sons, God hath sent forth the Spirit of his Son into your hearts, crying, Abba, Father. Wherefore thou art no more a servant, but a son; and if a son, then an heir of God through

Jesus Christ" (Gal. 4:6-7), even "joint heirs with Christ" (Rom. 8:17).

Thus we see that in Christian experience a new relationship is established on the basis of a new kind of life given by God. The life of God is in the life of man. God comes to man in Christ. There comes the consciousness of a new companionship. This is a historical fact but it is more—it is a present spiritual reality. It is a fact in human history, but it is also a fact in human experience. Thus we go forth not just with a "doctrine" but with "good news"; not just with an idea of God but in a new relationship with God. Man may know God for himself, directly and with his whole self. Here is the solution to man's problem; here is the way out of his predicament.

Christian Experience Means Salvation

The term salvation is a broad term and has many meanings which are to be determined by the context. It is used here to mean God's work of saving men.

Sin brings separation. Salvation brings communion. Sin is enmity. Christ brings reconciliation. Sin is guilt; salvation is pardon or forgiveness. Sin is defilement; salvation means cleansing. Sin brings disintegration of life and personality; Christ brings integration or wholeness of personality. Sin is spiritual death; salvation through Christ is life.

Other words of the same or similar meaning as, or included in, or concomitant to, the word salvation are such expressions as reconciliation, redemption, deliverance, conversion, justification, sanctification, remission, forgiveness, pardon, regeneration, the new birth, finding God, accepting Christ, the baptism of the Spirit, filled with the Spirit, perfect love. For our purpose we need not be technical. We shall use these words to help us to gain and give insights into the totality of

Concerning Christian Experience and Life 63

what God does for men in Jesus Christ in bringing them back into right relationship with himself, with themselves, and with other selves.

Salvation is from something to something. Man is to be saved *from* sin. He is to be saved *to* God. It is a taking away of the wrong and a giving and receiving of the right. It is both negative and positive, and the negative is always in order that we may come to the positive. Salvation is being converted from sin to holiness. The lost is found. Cleansing is in order that the heart may be filled. Conversion is turning *from;* it is also turning *toward.* The house is not only swept and garnished, but occupied. It is a change of allegiance from the bondage of sin to freedom in Christ. We are to be saved *from* something, *to* something, *for* something.

Christ is the Savior. "Thou shalt call his name Jesus, for he shall save his people from their sins" (Matt. 1:21). A savior, if he really is one, saves. And this is precisely what Christ does.

Saviorhood is of the very essence of Christ, and salvation is the universal need of humanity. This we believe and this we can join even with angels in proclaiming, "Fear not, for, behold, I bring you good tidings of great joy, which shall be to all people. For unto you is born this day in the city of David, a Savior, which is Christ the Lord" (Luke 2:10-11). This Savior which was once born in Bethlehem can be eternally born in us.

Salvation is saving from sin. Salvation must be thought of in terms of moral and spiritual reality if it is to have meaning. It must take into consideration sin and guilt on the part of man, and judgment and grace on the part of God. "He was manifested to take away our sins" (I John 3:5). He "gave himself for our sins, that he might deliver us from this present evil world" (Gal. 1:4). Jesus saves from the guilt of sin, the power of sin, the pollution of sin, the penalty of sin.

Salvation is forgiveness of sin. Forgiveness is one of the great truths of the Bible and one of the vital realities of Christian experience. The problem of the universe, let it be reiterated, is the problem of sin. In Christ there is forgiveness of sin. Forgiveness is a miracle of grace, for there is no forgiveness in nature; nature always exacts her "pound of flesh," Shylocklike. Nature's law is "reap what you sow." Forgiveness is the removal of the guilt of sin and the remission of the penalty of sin. This man needs, and this God provides, and this the Bible clearly teaches.

This forgiveness God gives through Christ out of the riches of his grace. "In whom we have redemption through his blood, the forgiveness of sins, according to the richness of his grace" (Epr. 1:7). "Even the forgiveness of sins" (Col. 1:14).

"Blessed is the man whose transgression is forgiven, whose sin is covered" (Ps. 32:1). He is blessed or happy because the ghosts of the past are laid low and the fear of judgment is taken away.

Salvation means restoration of holiness. Saving from sin means saving to holiness. Holiness is more than a showy piousness, or a sentimental self-righteousness, or a holier-than-thou hypocrisy. It is a power, a condition of being, and a life. Holiness is wholeness, purity, sincerity, dedication. More will be said on this in other sections.

Justification by Faith

The word justification is used here not to set it over against the use of the word salvation, for it is included in that term. Nor is it set over against the

Concerning Christian Experience and Life

concepts of forgiveness, remission, regeneration, or conversion, for it is simply another aspect of God's work of grace in Christian experience and is concomitant with the experience which these words describe. But justification by faith was a dominant emphasis of the Protestant Reformation because it is so prominent in the New Testament, and it needs to be a focus of our faith and message today.

Forgiveness, pardon, and remission are somewhat synonymous with the word and idea of justification. Justification is a judicial term, as is pardon. They all have reference to our relationship to God, to our standing before him. When we are forgiven, pardoned, when our sins are remitted, or we are justified, we not only stand in right relationship to God but also to man. This change we call regeneration or the new birth.

Since God is just, and since "all have sinned, and come short of the glory of God" (Rom. 3:23), all need to be justified. The ground of our faith for justification is in Jesus Christ and the price he paid for our salvation. What Jesus did on the cross is the basis for God's forgiveness: "That he might be just, and the justifier of him which believeth" (vs. 26). Because of this we may be "justified freely by his grace, through the redemption that is in Christ Jesus" (vs. 24).

"Therefore being justified by faith, we have peace with God through our Lord Jesus Christ" (5:1). It is this justification in the sight of God which makes salvation real and true. Justification is the work, not of man, but of God.

Sanctification by the Spirit.

This, too, is included in the purpose of redemption as it is set forth in the New Testament. It is here being considered as that operation of God's grace in the hearts and lives of his believing and dedicated children, which purifies their hearts and lives by the indwelling power of the Holy Spirit. In considering this, it may be well to consider something of the work of the Holy Spirit in general in God's redemptive purpose.

The work of the Holy Spirit. The Holy Spirit is the third Person in the concept of God as a holy Trinity. He is always regarded as personal. So anything we think of as the work of the Spirit is the work of a Person.

He has always been at work even in creation, for "the Spirit of God moved upon the face of the waters" (Gen. 1:2). In the Old Testament period he came to men on special occasions to accomplish the work of God in and through them. He came to Jesus in the hour of his baptism in the form of a dove.

In the work of saving men, it is the Spirit who convinces and convicts of sin: "When he is come, he will reprove the world of sin" (John 16:8). He works in the process of the new birth: "born of water and of the Spirit" (3:5). He witnesses to sonship when one is born again: "The Spirit itself beareth witness with our spirit, that we are the children of God" (Rom. 8:16). He reveals the Son to us even as the Son revealed the Father: "He shall take of mine, and shall show it unto you" (John 16:15). He teaches and guides the believing child of God: "He shall teach you all things, and bring all things to your remembrance, whatsoever I have said unto you" (14:26); "He will guide you into all truth" (16:13). All these he did for the first disciples, and all these he does for his children in all ages.

The Spirit fills with his Presence. Before Jesus went away he promised to send the Holy Spirit in full meas-

Concerning Christian Experience and Life

ure and as an abiding presence. "It is expedient for you that I go away; for if I go not away, the Comforter will not come unto you; but if I depart, I will send him unto you" (John 16:7). In giving the church its work to do Jesus said, "Ye shall receive power after that the Holy Ghost is come upon you: and ye shall be witnesses unto me both in Jerusalem, and in all Judea, and in Samaria, and unto the uttermost part of the earth" (Acts 1:8).

In obedience to his command, and with faith in his promise, his followers tarried in Jerusalem, waiting for the fulfillment. "When the day of Pentecost was fully come, they were all with one accord in one place. . . . And they were all filled with the Holy Ghost" (2:1-4). When the conversion of the gathered multitude followed Peter's preaching on that same day, Peter reiterated the promise of the same Spirit to them: "Repent and be baptized every one of you in the name of Jesus Christ for the remission of sins, and ye shall receive the gift of the Holy Ghost. For the promise is unto you, and to your children, and to all that are afar off, even as many as the Lord your God shall call" (vss. 38-39). Later when other thousands were converted we read, "They were all filled with the Holy Ghost" (4:31). Thus it continues in the life of the early church as recorded in Acts and the Epistles.

The Spirit cleanses with his Presence. This work of divine infilling is also called sanctification. In referring to the experience of the believers on the day of Pentecost and in explaining what happened there, Peter said, "Giving them the Holy Ghost, even as he did unto us; and put no difference between us and them, purifying their hearts by faith" (Acts 15:8-9).

Jesus prayed, in his high-priestly prayer, as recorded in John 17, for the sanctification of his people. That prayer was for the church—his people—not the world. It was for that church which he was to "purchase with his own blood" that he prayed. Therefore, we are ready to hear Paul say, "Christ also loved the church and gave himself for it; that he might sanctify and cleanse it with the washing of water by the word, that he might present it to himself a glorious church, not having spot, or wrinkle, or any such thing; but that it should be holy and without blemish" (Eph. 5:25-27). A sanctified church means a church whose members are dedicated, set apart for the service of God, cleansed, and filled with the Indwelling Presence, and hence has power. This promised power is the power of purity, of holy love, of dedicated purpose, of oneness of faith and effort.

The Spirit works by giving himself to men as men give themselves to him. As man gives himself in surrender and dedication and consecration, God responds by giving the Spirit, who gives power for life and witness.

If every child of God will obey Paul's call in Romans 12:1, "I beseech you therefore, brethren, by the mercies of God, that ye present your bodies a living sacrifice, holy, acceptable unto God, which is your reasonable service," we would find that Christian living would be lifted to a higher plane, and there would be a great upsurge in power for service.

MAN'S PART IN BECOMING A CHRISTIAN

In the analysis of God's work in bringing men into this new life in Christ frequent reference was made to man's part in the process. God's work in man's heart is conditioned by what man makes it possible for God to do.

God has taken the initiative in the saving process

Concerning Christian Experience and Life 69

by sending his Son as Savior and his Spirit to convict men of sin. God works through the revelation which he has given of himself in his Word. But man must respond to what God does, and then he will find God responding by doing what he has promised to do in his Word.

Man's response to the convicting and drawing of the Spirit is most commonly spoken of as repentance and faith.

Repentance

The one who feels deeply guilty will deeply repent. As the Spirit of conviction takes hold man responds by being sorry for his sin, by turning from sin, by "changing his mind" and his whole attitude toward sin. For repentance is "to think again," "to change one's mind," "to turn about." This "mind-changing" must be moral and spiritual if it is to have Christian significance. It is changing one's mind about sin, about life itself, about God and his will for man. It issues in a changed life. It is "turning about" from a self-centered life to a God-centered life. It is a turning *from* something and a turning *to* something—from sin and to God.

Real repentance is never a sorrow unto despair. It is shot through and through with hope. "Godly sorrow worketh repentance to salvation not to be repented of" (II Cor. 7:10). True repentance leads the person to a clearing of the past by confessing his sin to God and making his wrongs right with others as far as that is possible. It causes one to have the spirit that characterized Zaccheus who, when he came into the holy presence of Jesus, wanted to straighten up his life by restoring ill-gotten gains, thus making reparation.

This repentance is personal sorrow for personal sin against a personal God. But it must be a door which leads to a changed life. It is because man repents that God can forgive and that man can receive forgiveness.

Desire to know God must lead to decision to take the steps necessary to knowing him. That which has broken the relationships of life must be put out of the way.

"Whosoever shall call upon the name of the Lord shall be saved" (Rom. 10:13) is the promise. It is by obedience and prayer that a foundation is laid for faith that God forgives and saves.

Faith

To stress these two steps, repentance and faith, is not to set them over against each other, or to say which precedes the other, for they go along together in many respects. It may be said that one will not repent unless he has some faith that God will forgive. But on the other hand, one cannot have faith unless he repents. The two together are to be understood simply as the moving of the soul toward God.

Faith is repentance made hopeful. Faith means faith in God as revealed in Jesus Christ. It is always personal faith in a personal God which brings salvation. "To as many as received him, to them gave he power to become children of God."

The faith which brings man into right relation with God is the repentant sinner's perfect personal trust in Jesus Christ as his Savior from sin, for the process is "repentance toward God and faith toward our Lord Jesus Christ" (Acts 20:21). Faith is more than mumbling a formula or mouthing a creed. Believing means choosing, deciding, committing, giving one's self to God who in response to man's giving gives Himself. It is faith in a living Christ, in whom, and in whom alone, is salvation. He gives his saving help to shattered, frustrated, thwarted, sinful men. Faith is believing the good news that life can be made new—can be made over again. Faith is man's opening of his heart to God by repentance and submission to the will of God.

The call of God is "repent ye, and believe the gospel," the good news. "Repent and be baptized every one of you in the name of Jesus Christ" (Acts 2:38) was the way Peter answered the question, "What shall we do?" Paul answered the question of the Philippian jailer by saying, "Believe on the Lord Jesus Christ, and thou shalt be saved" (16:31). Peter said "Repent"; Paul said "Believe." Which was right? Both were; for the two go together, and there cannot be one in the fullest sense without the other. This applies to "every creature": "Go ye into all the world, and preach the gospel to every creature. He that believeth and is baptized shall be saved" (Mark 16:15-16).

All this requires humility, for only he who becomes like a little child can enter the kingdom of heaven. See Matthew 18:3.

THE CHRISTIAN LIFE

Christian life grows out of Christian experience—an experience of Christ in one's life. From this heart throne Christ sways the scepter over the entire life.

A New Way of Life

"Therefore, if any man be in Christ, he is a new creature; old things are passed away; behold all things are become new" (II Cor. 5:17). This means new desires, new habits, new motives.

A Christian life means a consistent life. It is consistent with the profession we make, the name we bear. We bear the name of Christ and profess to be his followers. Paul could say, "Ye are witnesses, and God also, how holily and justly and unblamably we behaved ourselves among you" (I Thess. 2:10).

A Christian life means a holy life. "As he which has called you is holy, so be ye holy in all manner of conversation" (I Pet. 1:15). This means a life separated from the evil of the world. This means a clean, pure life.

A Christian life is an obedient life. This means obedience to the will of God as revealed in his Word and in the leadings of his Spirit. "If ye love me, keep my commandments."

A Christian life is one bearing the fruit of the Spirit. This is set forth by Paul in his letter to the Galatians, "The fruit of the Spirit is love, joy, peace, long-suffering, gentleness, goodness, faith, meekness, temperance" (Gal. 5:22-23).

The Christian life is a life of service. The Christian experience inculcates the widest sympathies and makes one's heart go out to all who have need of his help. The Christian throws himself enthusiastically into every effort which is for the welfare of his fellow man, especially in the work of saving men for God. The world needs the gospel and those who know Christ as Savior are the only ones who can take the good news to them.

"Son, go work today in my vineyard" is the call of Christ ringing out today.

A Life of Blessedness

The Christian life is a blessed life. The Beatitudes of Matthew 5:1-12 show the nature of the "blessed" or happy life. This scale, or standard, of happiness is set over against the world's concepts of happiness and has to do with the quality or spirit of life expressing itself in right action.

Concerning Christian Experience and Life 73

The promises of God are for all those who will believe them and build their lives upon them. This means a life of faith, not just in the promises but in the Promiser. We are not only justified by faith, but the Christian life is a life of faith—"The just shall live by faith" (Rom. 1:17).

We are told that if we will "seek . . . first the kingdom of God, and his righteousness, all these things shall be added unto" us (Matt. 6:33). The "all things" include the temporal and physical needs of man—food clothing, shelter, etc. God is concerned about all that concerns man, even his physical needs.

God's promises include physical healing for his children. The general promises of God are inclusive enough to take in divine healing even if there were no specific promises to that effect.

Divine healing is healing of disease, sickness, and affliction by the prayer of faith. Christ not only healed when he was here on earth, but he is "Jesus Christ, the same yesterday, today, and forever." Over and above all this, the Bible specifically promises healing in response to faith and obedience. "Is any among you afflicted? let him pray. . . . Is any sick among you? let him call for the elders of the church; and let them pray over him anointing him with oil in the name of the Lord: and the prayer of faith shall save the sick, and the Lord shall raise him up; and if he have committed sins, they shall be forgiven him" (Jas. 5:13-15).

The promises of God cover all the needs of his children of faith, both in the life which now is and in that which is to come.

The Christian life is a full life. The Christian life is a good way of life. It is a life of devotion to the will of God, of prayer, of reading the Bible, of communing with God, of fellowship, of worship, of service, and cooperation in the work of God.

The Christian life reaches into all areas of the inner life and out into all areas of life without.

The Christian way is an enlargement of life. It is not suppression of life, limitation of life, restriction of life, or repression of life. It is expansion, release, liberation, enlistment, unfolding, completion; all of life's powers having been redeemed are released and energized, then engaged in living and serving.

Summary

We have studied about God. He is. He is Creator, Sustainer, Provider—the ground and goal of all that is.

God has revealed himself in nature, in his created beings, and supremely in Christ, in whom he comes as Redeemer. Christ, by his atoning death, saves men. Christ came as "the way, the truth, and the life," and he came that we might have life, and that we might have it more abundantly.

The life which God would impart to us and which Christ came to give us is made effective in us by the Holy Spirit, the third person of the adorable Trinity. The Holy Spirit is the Spirit of life. He, by the new birth, brings new life. He brings life into right relation with God, who is life, and with others. The Holy Spirit cleanses and fills with power to live and witness. This is the Christian way of life.

Salvation is a new kind of life, a new order of life. It makes man a son of his heavenly Father. It is an "inwardness" of life as well as an "outwardness" of life.

This salvation is man's when by faith in God and repentance toward our Lord Jesus Christ, man receives Christ as his personal Savior.

Chapter V

CONCERNING THE CHURCH AND ITS MISSION

How could it be otherwise than that Christ who came to the world to make God known and to save men would, as a part of his redemptive work, build his church? For salvation not only brings men into right relations with God but into right relations the one to the other. The brotherhood of man goes right along with the Fatherhood of God. The church is the brotherhood of the redeemed and the organ of redemption. It is made up of "the saved," and those who are saved are seeking the salvation of others. One has spoken of the church as "the company of all those in every age who are joined to Christ in faith and love, and who labor for the ends which he seeks."

We want to look at the church both from the standpoint of the pattern as laid down in the teachings of the New Testament and as it functions in its work in the world.

What Is the Church?

The word "church" is used in a variety of ways in common everyday speech and in several ways in the Scriptures. Sometimes it is used in its universal or general sense as referring to all who are members of Christ's body—all the children of God's family. At other times it is used as referring to a local congregation of this family of God, or of God's people in a geographic section or area. Sometimes it is used in a purely denominational sense.

The origin of our English word "church" is not clear, but its New Testament counterpart is the Greek word *ecclesia*. The word is used in the four Gospels only twice, but it is found some 114 times in the rest of the New Testament. Its exact meaning and application are to be determined in every instance from its setting in the various passages. *Ecclesia* is a combination of a Greek root word and its prefixed preposition, meaning in a general sense "to call out." It was commonly used as referring to the body of citizens or representatives "called out" to legislative or other functions of the Greek city-state. Its application was made specific by adding the words "of God" so that it was "the *ecclesia* of God," or church of God.

Broadly and generally speaking in New Testament usage, the word *ecclesia* has two applications: the local congregation or assembly of the Christians in a given place; and the universal body of believers.

The Universal Church

In our teaching we have put a great deal of emphasis upon this phase of the church, and for the most part rightly so. In a day when the denominational concept of the church has obscured the truth of the meaning and function of the church, a clear understanding of the basic nature of the church is needed. A recognition by all Christians of the church as, most simply, the body of Christ, or family of God, and made up of all who are truly Christ's, would be a long step forward in bringing that unity for which Christ so sincerely prayed, as recorded in John 17.

Perhaps the figures of speech by which the church is set forth in the New Testament depicts more clearly the true nature of the church than does a study of the word *ecclesia* itself. Let us look at a number of these.

The church is "the body of Christ." As such it is made up of all who are members of Christ's body—all Christians. "For by one Spirit are we all baptized into one body" (I Cor. 12:13). "And gave him [Christ] to be the head over all things to the church, which is his body, the fullness of him that filleth all in all" (Eph. 1:22-23). "He is the head of the body, the church" (Col. 1:18). "Now hath God set the members every one of them in the body as it hath pleased him" (I Cor. 12:18). "So we being many, are one body in Christ, and every one members one of another" (Rom. 12:5). It can, in the light of these scriptures, be laid down as a simple fact that all true Christians are members of the one body, or church, of Christ. This we believe and this we proclaim.

The church is the family of God. It is that "whole family in heaven and earth" who bear the name and share the nature of their heavenly Father—the "Father of our Lord Jesus Christ."

It is that family into which one comes by being "born again" (John 3:3). All who are born of the Spirit are members of that family.

This means that the church is a brotherhood, a fellowship of all Christians. It is the fellowship of the redeemed, "the church of God, which he hath purchased with his own blood" (Acts 20:28).

God's purpose in redemption being to bring us into right relation with himself and with one another, we should expect the church to be the visible expression of the fellowship. Such it is. Such was it in the beginning, even before it had any formal organization, any ritual, any creed except faith in Christ and the "good news."

This concept of the church as a "fellowship" or family of God is absolutely basic to any proper understanding of the church. It arose by direct influence of Jesus Christ and grew out of his indwelling presence in the hearts and lives of those who came to know him in that new life of the Spirit which came by the "new birth." To be "born again" is to be born into the family of God, the church. To be "children of God" is to be brothers one of another. To be in fellowship with God is to be in fellowship with all who are in fellowship with Him. Servants of the Father, we serve one another. Loving him supremely we love one another. Knowing Christ, we want others to know him.

So the church is first and foremost a fellowship of all who are in the family of God—a fellowship of loving service. The church must move forward with Him as a new fellowship for the creation of a new humanity.

The church is the building of God. "Ye are God's building" (I Cor. 3:9). "Ye also, as lively stones, are built up a spiritual house, an holy priesthood, to offer up spiritual sacrifices, acceptable to God by Jesus Christ" (I Pet. 2:5). Each Christian is a part of this building "framed together" and "builded together for an habitation of God through the Spirit" (Eph. 2:21-22).

As a building, the church stands on a firm foundation, for Christ himself is its builder and it is builded upon a rock: "Upon this rock I will build my church" (Matt. 16:18). "Ye are . . . built upon the foundation of the apostles and prophets, Jesus Christ being the chief cornerstone" (Eph. 2:19-20). "Other foundation can no man lay than that is laid, which is Jesus Christ" (I Cor. 3:11).

Other figures of speech show what the church is. Not all need to be considered, but in the Bible the church is spoken of as the fold of God's sheep, of whom the Lord is the Good Shepherd. Into this fold or building

Jesus is the way of entrance: "I am the door; by me if any man enter in he shall be saved" (John 10:9). There is no other way of getting into God's church than by this door. One must be saved to be a member of the church: "The Lord added to the church daily such as should be saved" (Acts 2:47).

The church is the bride of Christ: "Come hither, I will show thee the bride, the Lamb's wife" (Rev. 21:9). "He that hath the bride is the bridegroom," or Christ (John 3:29).

It is the "city of my God, which is new Jerusalem, which cometh down out of heaven" (Rev. 3:12)—"the true sanctuary which the Lord pitched and not man" (Heb. 8:2).

These concepts of the church are basic. Emphasis needs to be put upon the foregoing concepts of the church as the universal body of believers, for all else that may need to be said about the church in its local or general functioning in the world needs to be in harmony with these basic concepts of the church.

The Local Congregation

The New Testament makes many references to the local church or congregation. In fact, in the majority of the 114 places where the word *ecclesia* is used the reference is to the local congregation. This is in harmony with the fact that the New Testament books, for the most part, were letters to particular local congregations of the church and were designed to meet the problems of those congregations; for instance, "the church which was in Jerusalem" (Acts 11:22); "the church which was at Antioch" (13:1); "the church of God which is at Corinth" (I Cor. 1:2). Many references clearly refer to local congregations; for example, Matthew 18:18, "Tell it to the church."

The relationship of the local church to the universal church is simply that of a part to the whole. The local church is a visible manifestation and functioning of the universal church. A local congregation is made up of those who in any given situation are joined to Christ and to one another by the ties of spiritual experience, who meet together for worship, edification, fellowship, instruction, and who work together for the extension of God's kingdom and the saving of a lost world.

Ideally, the local church would be made up of all Christians in a community, who because of common ties and common interests meet and work together. Membership in the universal church, or being a Christian, is by scriptural standards essential to membership in the local church; but association with the membership in a local group does not necessarily guarantee that one is a Christian. Ideally, it would be so, but in a local congregation the human element of association and recognition, formal or informal, enters in. This may mean that there are those who are associated with the local group and are by them recognized as members, who are not truly Christian. Then, too, because of this element of association and recognition on the human side, there may be Christians in the community, who are not members of a particular local manifestation of the church. Christian experience is and ought to be the basis of membership in the local congregation, but this does not of itself constitute one an actual member of any given congregation, but only a potential one.

Therefore, each Christian is a member of the congregation because of desire and identification on his part, and by reason of recognition on the part of the group. This recognition need not be in any particular form but is nevertheless a very definite thing. The

Concerning the Church and Its Mission 81

mutual understanding may not be according to any set form, but nevertheless it is real. In the Church of God movement different local churches have different ways of expressing such recognition.

Intercongregational and General Co-operation

In a real sense, you as a Christian are a member of the entire church of God, the whole family of God anywhere and everywhere. You are one with every Christian everywhere, and you will find many ways of expressing that fellowship wherever you are in association with other Christians. If you are visiting in a local congregation of the church of God other than your own congregation you will find there a spiritual oneness, and will feel at home, even though you will not be a part of its organizational activities. In meetings of various kinds where two or more churches meet together in youth rallies, religious education or missionary conventions and such like, you will be one with these kindred spirits. State, regional, national, and international conventions and camp meetings of various kinds are all practical expressions of spiritual fellowship. Ways are provided for working together with all Christians who are like-minded.

Not only do Christians as individuals co-operate with other Christians in such relationships, but in matters which concern the churches of any given geographical area the local congregations sustain a like relationship of fellowship and co-operative effort to each other. The Christian or congregation who isolates himself or itself and does not thus co-operate is missing much. In religious education, in youth work, in evangelism, in missions, in benevolence, and in other areas such co-operation is demanded for the highest good of each

Christian and the progress of the church in such sections or regions.

The nature of the church and of Christian experience implies a relationship of each Christian to other Christians and of local congregations to the general church. A local group which is in unity with other local groups and with the church generally will naturally want to co-operate with the church in order to share in the blessings and work of the church everywhere. There are needs to be met and work to be done which no local congregation of itself can do. "Go ye into all the world and preach the gospel to every creature" and "Go make disciples of all nations, teaching them to observe all things that I have commanded you, and lo, I am with you alway, even unto the end of the world"—how are we to carry out such marching orders except in co-operation with all who are like-minded?

The best way you as an individual Christian and your church as a local congregation can do some of the things which must be done in the work of taking the gospel to all the world is by association and co-operation with the total program of the total church.

The need for co-operation has led to the organizing of various agencies, sectional—by states or regions—national and international, which provide avenues of co-operative endeavor. These organizations are not of themselves sacrosanct or divine, but the work of taking the gospel to all the world is, and these are ways in which we may co-operate in doing just that. When better ways are found to do the work, then we are under obligation to use such better ways, but until other and better ways are set up, then each of us is under moral and spiritual obligation to work in the ways now available. Such working together is of itself an expression of practical unity and is the only way of getting some jobs done.

A state board of evangelism or of religious education, our national boards for carrying out the missionary, evangelistic, and educational tasks of the church, are not mandatory, but "preaching the gospel to every creature" and "teaching them to observe all things" are. If the ways which we have so far found are not the right ways at this time, then we are under obligation to find better ways. But until we do find other and better ways, let us use the means now available.

The Church and the Quest for Unity

From our previous consideration of what the church is, it is evident that the church is one in its basic structure. This is true whether it is thought of in its universal sense or as a local congregation. All true Christians are one in Christ, and as such are one in that fellowship which is the church. Yet, that something more is needed is also clearly evident. With this "something more" in mind, let us look at the situation.

Unity of the Spirit

A deep unity, in fact, now exists. It is involved in the very nature of Christian experience and in the nature of the church as the body of Christ, the family of born-again ones, the city of God, the household of faith, the bride of Christ. Christian unity does not have to be created. It cannot be voted into being. It is a work of the Spirit of God.

Christians are one in spiritual experience. The church is one. Jesus built only one: "I will build my church, and the gates of hell shall not prevail against it" (Matt. 16:18). It is made up of all who are born of the Spirit, "for by one Spirit are we all baptized into one body" (I Cor. 12:13).

Unity is set forth in the New Testament as a fundamental of the church. It is the "church of God." The words "church of God" are more than a name, in the shallower meaning of the word "name." It is called or named the church of God because it is the church of God. See such passages as Acts 20:28; I Corinthians 1:2; 10:32; 15:9; II Corinthians 1:1; Galatians 1:13.

This may seem to some like an overinsistence upon a very simple and generally accepted fact. But, as a matter of fact, this concept is basic to any consideration of the church's quest for a more nearly complete and functioning unity. For whatever else may be said about the church, as to the full unity for which Christ prayed, recorded in John 17, must be in harmony with, and must grow out of, this basic, simple truth—the church is the body of Christ, the family of believers, the beloved community, and is made up of all Christians—all who have been born again and are walking in the light which God gives.

The acceptance of this plain truth will not solve all the problems which arise in the church's quest for a full and functioning unity, but it does provide a basis for such a quest; and without the acceptance of this basic fact unity will not be found.

Unity in Christ is not enough. "Something more" is needed. What is this "something more"?

A Functioning Unity Is Needed

For a unity manifest to the world Jesus prayed, for this he gave his life, and for this the Spirit of God is working in the hearts of Christians everywhere today.

In Jesus' high-priestly prayer, recorded at length in John 17, is an earnest plea for his church, his fol-

Concerning the Church and Its Mission

lowers. He made it clear that he was praying for all who were then his followers and for all who would follow afterward. "Neither pray I for these alone, but for them also which shall believe on me through their word; that they all may be one; as thou, Father, art in me, and I in thee, that they also may be one in us: that the world may believe that thou hast sent me" (John 17:20-21).

Here it is the prayer of Jesus that the unity which is spiritual may be expressed in such a way that "the world may believe." Here the believing of the world is conditioned upon a oneness which will enable them to see and know that God sent his Son to be the Savior of the world. That unity which is spiritual needs to be made visible. Everything that hinders an adequate expression of that unity for which Christ prayed must be discarded, and the church must work together in getting the gospel to the world in a way that will convince the world.

Division is contrary to God's purpose. Divisions, denominational or personal, are condemned by the Word of God. The Spirit of God is not a sectarian spirit. Sectarianism, wherever it is found, is unchristian. The divine standard is "that there be no divisions among you" (I Cor. 1:10) and that there "should be no schism in the body" (12:25).

The denominational expression of the church must somehow be discarded, and the things which separate into different denominations must be swallowed up in a great urge and surge toward unity.

Unity of the Spirit must issue in a unity of faith. There was a visible unity in the early church: "The multitude of them that believed were of one heart and one soul" (Acts 4:32). To maintain this unity Paul wrote, "I therefore, the prisoner of the Lord, beseech you that ye walk worthy of the vocation wherewith ye are called, with all lowliness and meekness, with longsuffering, forbearing one another in love; endeavoring to keep the unity of the Spirit in the bonds of peace" (Eph. 4:1-3). This unity of the Spirit, if it is kept, will lead to a unity of faith or belief. It is to be kept "till we all come in the unity of the faith" (vs. 13), and this in turn will produce a people who will "stand fast in one spirit, with one mind striving together for the faith of the gospel" (Phil. 1:27).

These aspects of unity—unity of Spirit, of faith, and of purpose or work—are not to be thought of as successive stages of unity but as aspects or phases of unity always in the process of being achieved—a continuing and continuous quest.

This unity of the Spirit and faith must be a working unity. Oneness in Christ is not enough. Oneness in doctrine is not enough. All Christians must work together in the one task which God has given his church to do. Unity of the Spirit, unity of faith or message, and unity of purpose and action—all these are needed if the church is to fulfill its mission in the world.

Christian people everywhere need to join this quest and movement for unity. Every Christian needs to see the purpose for which Christ wants unity, the end toward which the unity of the church is a means. This will become increasingly evident as we think even for a moment about the mission of the church.

The Mission of the Church

There is not space here to say all that God has in mind for his church, but all that he has for his church to do finds its charter in the words of its founder: "Go ye into all the world, and preach the gospel to every creature" (Mark 16:15). "Go . . . teach all nations . . ." (Matt. 28:19). "Ye shall be witnesses unto me" (Acts 1:8).

The mission of the church is varied—the worship of God, the edification of one another, and taking the gospel to the world.

The Church's Mission Is to Edify Its Members

A sense of obligation to help one another motivates the life of the church. We see the first disciples of Jesus doing this even while he was yet with them. Even Jesus recognized this principle of edification through fellowship. He chose twelve "that they might be with him" as well as "that he might send them forth." The hundred and twenty gathered with "one accord in one place" after Jesus went away. When the three thousand were converted on Pentecost "they continued steadfastly" not only in the doctrine, but in "fellowship and the breaking of bread," which was a meal of fellowship. "They continued daily with one accord in the temple, and breaking bread from house to house." All this is found in Acts 2.

This was a practical fellowship of mutual care and concern, even to having "all things common" (Acts 4:32 ff.). Later seven men were appointed to administer their program of helpfulness. See Acts 6.

One of the concerns of the church today is the perpetuation of itself for the propagation of the gospel and the accomplishing of God's redemptive purpose. The church is the continuing agency of the ongoing redemptive purpose of God. In view of its work the church must build itself up in love and in all the qualities that will make it a more effective agency for the worship of God and the evangelization of men.

The Church's Mission Is the Worship of God

In worship the church not only glorifies God but builds itself up. Worship is not so much for the sake of the One worshiped as for the one worshiping. The worship of God is one of the most direct and purposive functions of the church, since it is one of the inevitable expressions of the Christian life. It has its basis in the very nature of Christian experience as it relates one to God and to his fellow Christians. Public or corporate worship arises out of the social nature of man and of Christian experience. The church is a divine-human fellowship, and public worship is one of the basic expressions of that fellowship. One aspect of that fellowship is fellowship with God; another is the fellowship with each other of all who are in fellowship with God.

In this worship insights are gained, the will of God is discerned, and resources of strength are found. Inspiration is kindled for Christian life and service.

The Mission of the Church Is to Herald the Evangel

The church has a message for the world. It has a message for all the world. It has a message for every one in the world. The primary task of the church is to give the good news to men.

The church has a message for men who are lost. Men in sin must know that there is salvation from sin. The church in its message must come to grips with the sin problem, in human life and human society.

Men must not only see that they are lost but that they can be saved. Man must not only see his sin but he must see a forgiving and redeeming Christ. Men must see what God has done and is doing about sin. The "good news" is that in Jesus Christ God is at work reconciling the world unto himself.

Concerning the Church and Its Mission

God has done and is doing something. The gospel is not of man's devising; it is God's deed. It is the good news of God's act and God's intervention in behalf of and for man's redemption, individually and severally, here and hereafter.

But the church is the ongoing agency of that redemptive purpose of God.

The church has a message for Christians. Christians need to grow. They grow by making greater room in their lives for God and the truths of his Word. Christians need a continually deepening life in the Spirit. They need abundant life. They need power to witness by life and deed. They need power for witnessing effectively in working to save others. Many need the sanctifying power of the Holy Spirit.

The sick need God's healing touch. Many do not know of these and many other privileges which are a part of their rich inheritance in Jesus Christ. It is the mission of those who know these things to let others know about them.

The church has a message for our confused world. Every problem that faces the world today is directly or indirectly a moral problem. The chaos and confusion and sin of our day—the oppression and injustice and greed and lust for power—the false ideologies and paganisms—have their only remedy in the principles of the good news about God as revealed in Christ Jesus.

The church alone is custodian of a message which alone can bring fellowship, brotherhood, and world peace.

When the church can go to the world as one church with the one message, then we may begin to expect "one world."

This is one of the most tremendous reasons for the

church to help answer the prayer of Christ for its oneness—"that the world may know."

The church has a message for a hesitant and divided church. While the world gropes its way in darkness, the church also seems to be groping for a way out—hesitant and confused. There is a way out. The way out is a church of power, spiritual power, a power that will come as the church rediscovers the source of its power. Here again one must think of the need for the unity of the church.

The Church and Its Symbolic Ceremonies

A symbolic ceremony is a visible presentation of spiritual ideas or experiences in some outer and sacred form.

There has been much misunderstanding and difference of opinion concerning the meaning of such observances, both as to what they are and as to how they are to be observed. But there has been quite general agreement that the church is under divine command to observe such expressions of its faith. Almost all bodies of people have recognized the Lord's Supper in some way. Baptism has been quite generally practiced, though there has been widespread and vigorous disagreement both as to its purpose and the mode of its observance. The rite of foot washing has not been so generally recognized and practiced in the history of the church. Even in the New Testament it is mentioned much less frequently than the other two ceremonies.

Though such observances are few and simple, yet they are spiritually significant. They symbolize deep spiritual experiences on the part of the individual Christian; and as ceremonial observances in the church they represent the three basic relationships of the

Concerning the Church and Its Mission 91

Christian—to the world, to God, and to his fellow Christians.

Baptism Symbolizes Initial Christian Experience

Christ, in his last commission to his disciples, commanded them, "Go ye into all the world, and preach the gospel to every creature. He that believeth and is baptized shall be saved" (Mark 16:15-16). Here baptism is closely associated with believing. Peter urged it on the Day of Pentecost. "Then they that gladly received his word were baptized" (Acts 2:41). Many other references could be cited from all parts of the New Testament.

Baptism of itself is not a saving rite; rather it is the symbol of God's cleansing of the human heart. It is an outward symbol of an inner work of God's grace. It is a testimony to the world that the one being baptized is dead to sin and to the evil world and has been resurrected to a new life.

Baptism is for believers: "He that believeth and is baptized"; "Repent and be baptized"; "They were baptized, both men and women" (Acts 8:12).

Baptism by immersion is the consistent teaching of the Word. Immersion symbolizes the burial of one who is dead to sin, and coming up out of the water pictures the resurrection to newness of life. "Therefore we are buried with him by baptism into death: that like as Christ was raised up from the dead by the glory of the Father, even so we also should walk in newness of life" (Rom. 6:4).

The Lord's Supper Symbolizes Communion with God

As believers gather at the table of the Lord they testify by taking the wine and the bread that they are partaking of His life and are in sacred union with God through Christ. Christ commanded this, saying, "This do in remembrance of me." Recalling how His body was broken and his blood spilled, the communicant makes new decisions and strengthens his dedications.

Matthew records simply: "As they were eating, Jesus took bread, and blessed it, and brake it, and gave it to his disciples, and said, Take, eat; this is my body. And he took the cup, and gave thanks, and gave it to them, saying, Drink ye all of it; for this is my blood of the new testament, which is shed for many for the remission of sins" (26:26-28).

Footwashing Symbolizes Humble Service

Our Master himself gave us this example and made it a symbol of humble service the one to the other. The record is in John 13. In Jesus' example we see the greatness of service. We can do no better than to look at Jesus' own words and let them speak to us what they will. "Know ye what I have done to you? Ye call me Master and Lord; and ye say well; for so I am. If I then, your Lord and Master, have washed your feet; ye also ought to wash one another's feet. For I have given you an example, that ye should do as I have done to you. Verily, verily, I say unto you, The servant is not greater than his lord; neither he that is sent greater than he that sent him. If ye know these things, happy are ye if ye do them" (vss. 12-17).

Symbols May Be Empty Forms

Symbols may be charged with spiritual meanings and will be as long as the substance creates the form. But when the thing symbolized is not a reality, then the form becomes mere formality.

Not as hard and fast legalistic requirements, not in the letter but in the Spirit, these ceremonies are to

Concerning the Church and Its Mission 93

be used. They are not ends in themselves; they do not procure Christian experience. But when in a spirit of loyalty, and because love prompts and the culture of the soul demands, and as expressions of spiritual reality, these ceremonies are entered into, then the words of Jesus are proved true, "Happy are ye if ye do them." Then the symbols become a means of spiritual uplift to the individual and a testimony to others of those basic relationships of the Christian life—toward the world, toward God, and toward each other.

Summary

Believing in God as revealed in Jesus Christ and in the redemptive work of Christ which makes men and women Christians and produces right relations between them, we have the necessary basis for believing in and proclaiming the church as the visible expression of Christian fellowship here and now.

The church is, most simply, the fellowship of those who are children of God. It is the family of God, a fellowship. It is made up of the "born again," born from above. It is "the church of God which he hath purchased with his own blood" (Acts 20:28).

This church is one so far as its basic structure and spiritual life are concerned. But it is not enough that all Christians are spiritually one. There must be a practical, functioning unity. There can be no real, functioning unity except upon the basis of actual spiritual unity, but unity must go beyond this basic unity if the church is to be the kind of church that can do God's work in the world today. Jesus prayed for a functioning unity. We must help answer his prayer. "Neither pray I for these alone, but for them also which shall believe on me through their word; that they all may be one; as thou, Father, art in me, and I in thee, that they also may be one in us: that the world may believe that thou hast sent me" (John 17:20-21).

This unity must be the kind and degree of unity that will enable the church to give a convincing and convicting witness to the world so that our world may be saved.

Chapter VI
CONCERNING THE ASSURED HOPE OF THE FUTURE

No Christian affirmation and no Christian proclamation would be complete without something being said about the assured hope of the future. This is true both as to the fulfillment of life for the individual and as to the accomplishment of God's purpose in his Kingdom. This purpose is evident in the creation and becomes increasingly evident in a study of God's redemptive purpose.

Christian hope, along with Christian faith and Christian love, endures. We cannot segregate one from the other, for it is faith in the power of love which gives that assured hope.

In the full fruition of Christian hope many events and incidents are involved, but all derive meaning and significance from the part they play in the final accomplishment of the purposes of God in a new creation.

Involved in that assured hope is a firm faith that the future here in time is in God's hands—a faith in his superintending providence that causes us to exclaim, "We know that all things work together for good to them that love God" (Rom. 8:28)—a faith that even beyond death there is life, and that in the "sweet by and by" God will be all in all.

In this chapter we shall look at the Christian's hope of immortality; at the kingdom of God here and now and at its consummation in the eternal kingdom when

Jesus comes again to deliver up the Kingdom to the Father, at which time will be the resurrection of the dead and the general judgment, with punishment of the wicked and reward of the righteous.

GOD'S PURPOSE FOR THE INDIVIDUAL ACCOMPLISHED

The soul of man is immortal, or never dying. This is true both of the wicked and the righteous. But there is a quality of life which the Christian has—Jesus spoke of it as "eternal life,"—which begins here and persists forever in the life beyond death. It might indeed be said that the wicked *exist* forever and the righteous *live* forever.

A sense of expectancy has always characterized vital religion. There is always something to which to press forward. The sense of present privilege is not at all inconsistent with the expectation of future glory. The two are not mutually exclusive but each complements and completes the other.

The Christian hope of immortality is the assurance of continuing fellowship with God, which fellowship is a reality here and now. The doctrine of immortality is the expression of Christian insight into the mystery of the future. It is based upon such a sense of the meaning and worth-whileness of life and of God's work and purpose as makes the future meaningful and immortality and continuance desirable as well as possible.

Eternal life is not just life after death; it is a quality of life that begins here and continues in eternity. It is that life of which Jesus spoke, "This is life eternal, that they might know thee, the only true God, and Jesus Christ, whom thou hast sent" (John 17:3)

Faith in the Future

The Christian has more than a hope of the future—his is a firm faith in the future which is first of all a faith in God. It is faith in God the Eternal that gives the basis of faith in the future.

Believing in God we believe in his undying love, his divine wisdom, his eternal power, and his glorious and gracious purpose for man. Would this God create life and all these moral and spiritual personal values only to let death snuff them out?

Believing in life and in the conservation of all spiritual values, we say with Tennyson:

> Thou wilt not leave us in the dust:
> Thou madest man, we know not why;
> He thinks he was not made to die;
> And Thou hast made him: Thou art just.

"If a Man Die—"

Death is always contemporary, and no year goes by for any of us without regretted partings. Furthermore, all of us are under sentence of death. This sentence may be indefinitely reprieved, but there is only a step between us and the grave. To all of the thoughtful comes Job's question, not "will a man die" but "shall he live again?"

Death is not only a certain fact; it is a tragic fact. It is not tragic just in the sense that it is sad, but in the proper sense of tragic: it is irresolvable, irreconcilable, an inexplicable tension in life—in conflict with life. That is, it is all of this if death is final; if death has the last word. It is a contradiction of life in terms of human personality. But death does not have the last word. Life is stronger than death.

Over against the natural fear of death we put faith

in our Lord Jesus Christ who triumphed over death. His victory over death has robbed death of its sting and the grave of its victory so that we can sing with Paul, "Thanks be to God, which giveth us the victory through our Lord Jesus Christ" (I Cor. 15:57).

Jesus faced his own death, insofar as its personal consequences were concerned, as calmly as though he were merely going into another room in the house: "In my Father's house are many mansions"; "I go . . . I will come again"; "Let not your heart be troubled: ye believe in God, believe also in me" (John 14:1-3).

This belief in an endless life gives faith not only for the future, but for here and now, for it gives the victory over one of life's haunting fears—the fear of death; this faith delivers "them who through fear of death were all their lifetime subject to bondage" (Heb. 2:15).

"Shall He Live Again?"

There is a surer answer to Job's question than all our aspirations, longings, reasonings. Jesus himself gives the answer: "Because I live, ye shall live also" (John 14:19).

From *Toward Understanding God* I quote, "There may be times when this question, 'If a man die, shall he live again?' holds only speculative interest. But there are other times when it holds practical interest. Life is sweet now, but what of the days when our earthly life is almost gone? And what of the dear dead who have gone on before? Has the Author of our being found nothing better for the goodness and strength and beauty of life than to blot it out? Are fidelity and purity and love so lightly esteemed by Him? I cannot believe it. So long as my heart testifies to a Moral Order, august, cosmic, eternal; so long as I can see the divine glory shining in the face of Jesus Christ; so long will I believe the testimony of my heart, that 'because he lives, we shall live also' and live always. This belief is a spiritual achievement, rather than a process of logic or a demonstration of science."

GOD'S PURPOSE FOR THE RACE ACCOMPLISHED

God's purpose of redemption is not only for the redemption of the individual; his purpose is also a social purpose—the redemption of the race. His purpose is not only a kingdom—a kingdom of "righteousness peace and joy in the Holy Ghost"—here and now, but also an eternal kingdom of unending peace and joy, which shall last while the ages shall roll.

The Complete Redemption of the Race

God's purpose now is that, by this process of redemption which we have been studying, he may have a new race of holy human beings with whom he may hold loving fellowship. This is one way of stating God's purpose in creating man in the first place—that he might have a race of holy human beings upon whom he could bestow his love and who in turn could reciprocate that love by obeying him and serving one another. Sin came and that purpose was thwarted—but not defeated. God set himself to redeem out of that old race a new race of holy human beings with whom he could hold loving fellowship, and who in turn would be in fellowship with him and with one another. This he is now doing by saving men, binding them into fellowship both with himself and with one another in the church, which is the fellowship of the redeemed. His church is the present expression of that purpose. That purpose will be fully realized in the future when his redemptive work is complete, and all his family are with him and one another in that eternal home—

the new heaven and the new earth wherein dwelleth righteousness.

The Church Triumphant

Another way of stating the purpose of God is to state it as the final triumph of the church. The church has been spoken of as the church militant and the church triumphant.

The church militant, now doing her redemptive work, will be the church triumphant when her work of redemption is done. Now she confronts the lost world—a world in sin, a world alienated from God—with the claims of the gospel of Jesus Christ. This "good news" is that Jesus Christ is the only "way, the truth, and the life." In Him alone is salvation. When God's purpose of redemption is accomplished, then the church militant will share with him and be the church triumphant.

The Consummation of His Kingdom

The Kingdom has already come. It came when Jesus came the first time. But its consummation is yet to be. To grasp fully what is meant by this statement about the consummation of his kingdom we may need to consider for a moment what his kingdom is. The word "kingdom" is, in the Scriptures, used in a number of ways and with varied meanings, the meaning in any instance to be drawn from the context in which the word is used.

First, the word "kingdom" is used to express God's rule in a general way over his entire creation. Nothing takes place in the world without God in a general way having a hand in it. Second, the Kingdom of Israel over which and in which God ruled, as set out in the Old Testament, was in a special sense the kingdom of

God before Christ. Third, there is the kingdom of grace, which is the rule of Christ in the hearts and lives of all Christians.

The kingdom of God is wherever God reigns, whether in human hearts or human society. It is the realm of grace into which men and women come by the process of the new birth (John 3:5). It is where God's will is done, even as Christ taught us to pray, "Thy kingdom come, thy will be done, on earth as it is in heaven" (Matt. 6:10). Wherever God's will is done there is his kingdom. "The kingdom of God . . . is righteousness, and peace, and joy in the Holy Ghost" (Rom. 14:17). "The kingdom of God is within you" (Luke 17:21).

But there is a kingdom of God yet future. For this kingdom of grace must issue in a kingdom of glory. The Messianic kingdom is the present phase of the eternal kingdom of God. It is one of those "last things" or "final things," the doctrine of which theology calls "eschatology."

It is that phase of the kingdom about which Jesus spoke in such passages as these: "Come, ye blessed of my Father, inherit the kingdom prepared for you from the foundation of the world" (Matt. 25:34); "then shall the righteous shine forth as the sun in the kingdom of their Father" (13:43).

Christian Eschatology

Maybe pardon needs to be begged for using this Greek word in a study like this, but it seems to be necessary if we are to grasp properly this concept of "the end" or of "last things." By "the end" is not meant just the end of the world or of this present age, as "the end of time."

Christian eschatology is the outcome of Christian redemption, the accomplishment of the purpose of God—its completion. God is now working toward the accomplishment of a specific purpose, or "end." Such a faith makes sense of things. Such a faith gives meaning to history, for history is not headed "down a blind alley" but is leading somewhere. The meaning of history lies beyond history. The meaning of time lies beyond time. God knows what that "somewhere" is and is working toward the accomplishment of that purpose.

Christian eschatology is a basis for faith in the future, for history is leading in the direction of that "far-off, divine event toward which the whole creation moves." Those ends or purposes were implicit in the beginning of human history, and they inhere in all God has done, is doing, and will do; and they will be fully realized at the last. So this we believe, and this we proclaim, that God's purpose will in the end be accomplished. Under whatever symbols it may be set forth in the Scriptures and however the events of the future may bring it about, God's purpose will be achieved. By seeing this end, or consummation, by faith, we see more clearly the ways in which God is now working in his church and kingdom to bring these purposes to full realization. Here is fulfillment.

This consummation may be stated in many ways. When God's redemptive purpose shall have been completed in the establishment of his eternal kingdom of glory, then that new race of holy human beings "shall know even as also we are known."

This is admirably summed up by Paul in I Corinthians 15:22-28: "For as in Adam all die, even so in Christ shall all be made alive. But every man in his own order: Christ the firstfruits; afterward they that are Christ's at his coming. Then cometh the end, when he shall have delivered up the kingdom to God, even the Father; when he shall have put down all rule and all authority and power. For he must reign, till he hath put all things under his feet. The last enemy that shall be destroyed is death. For he hath put all things under his feet. But when he saith all things are put under him, it is manifest that he is excepted which did put all things under him. And when all things shall be subdued unto him, then shall the Son also himself be subject unto him that put all things under him, that God may be all in all."

The foregoing passage gives not only a fitting conclusion to this section but a valuable springboard to the next sections, dealing with such subjects as the second coming of Christ, the general resurrection of the dead, the judgment, and final rewards and punishment. For all these are merely the means of the accomplishment of God's final purposes, the doctrine concerning which we call Christian eschatology.

THE RETURN OF CHRIST

That the Son of man is coming again to judge the world, vindicate righteousness, and consummate his kingdom in a transcendent sphere has been a vital element in the hope of Christians in all ages. It was clearly in the thinking and teaching of Jesus at his first advent that he would come again at the end of this age or dispensation to sit in judgment, to appraise the character of all men, to apportion their merit or demerit, to announce their destiny, and to overthrow evil and thus bring his kingdom to its supreme triumph and glory.

This We Believe ... This We Proclaim

The Teaching of the New Testament in General

It can be seriously questioned whether there is any reference in the Old Testament to a second advent of Jesus, as its forward look is concerned with his first advent. A recognition of this simple and self-evident fact would do away with many of the more fanciful ideas as to Christ's coming again. But in the New Testament, during his own ministry and in the life and teaching of his followers, references abound.

Scholars have estimated that reference to the return of Christ at the end of the age is made more than three hundred times in the New Testament, though it may seem strange to many that the popular expression "the second coming of Christ" is not found at all. Only once is it explicitly called Christ's appearing a "second time" (Heb. 9:28). Yet in one way or another the idea resounds throughout the New Testament, in such terms as "manifestation" or "appearance" or just simple "coming." Yet, let it be said that this teaching never stands alone as an isolated idea or truth but is always used to enforce ideas and teachings and exhortations that are related to the present gospel age. It is used to urge repentance, faith, patience, perseverance, readiness, diligence in service, and so on.

Whatever the symbolism or imagery used in referring to this "day of the Lord," the meaning is that this present age will be ended by some mighty manifestation of the personal presence and power of Jesus Christ when his redemptive purpose has been accomplished. We find references to "this far-off event toward which the whole creation moves" all the way from Jesus' own gracious "I will come again" of John 14:3 to the "even so, come, Lord Jesus" of Revelation 22:20, the next to the last verse in the Bible. Would it be de-

Concerning the Assured Hope of the Future

parting too much from our emphasis here to call attention to the last verse: "The grace of our Lord Jesus Christ be with you all. Amen"?

Jesus' Own Teaching

It is sometimes difficult to know just what "his coming," as Jesus himself referred to it, means, as sometimes he seems to speak of his coming as a process and sometimes as an event. He "comes" in the person and power of the Holy Spirit into the hearts of men, in the working of his church, and the building of his kingdom. The phrase is even used as in Matthew 10:23 where Jesus seemed to refer to his ministry then in Palestine. It is used as referring to his coming in power in his kingdom as on the Day of Pentecost and afterwards: "There be some standing here, which shall not taste of death, till they see the Son of man coming in his kingdom" (Matt. 16:28). But in most instances Jesus speaks of a coming again which is yet future even to us.

Only a few such references need to be cited here. "I go to prepare a place for you. And if I go and prepare a place for you, I will come again, and receive you unto myself; that where I am, there ye may be also" (John 14:2-3) is one of the most quoted of the many gracious promises Jesus gave. "The Son of man shall come in the glory of his Father with his angels; and then he shall reward every man according to his works" (Matt. 16:27).

Attention is called to the many parables of Jesus such as the wedding supper, the virgins, and others. Paul quotes Jesus when instituting the Lord's Supper as saying: "As often as ye eat this bread, and drink this cup, ye do show the Lord's death till he come" (I Cor. 11:26).

The "Blessed Hope" of the Early Church

Even as the heavenward-gazing disciples of our Lord stood by at Olivet, angels proclaimed His coming again: "Ye men of Galilee, why stand ye gazing up into heaven? this same Jesus, which is taken up from you into heaven, shall so come in like manner as ye have seen him go into heaven" (Acts 1:11). Jesus' coming again found a place in Peter's preaching right in the beginning of the work of the church: "He shall send Jesus . . . whom the heaven must receive until the times of restitution of all things" (3:20-21).

The return of Jesus was one of the truths which brought hope when all else failed and the early Christians found no earthly basis for hope in this present world: "Looking for that blessed hope and the glorious appearing of the great God and our Savior Jesus Christ" (Titus 2:13).

Fact and Speculation

There are few doctrines about which there has been more useless, and sometimes harmful, speculation than about our Lord's coming again. The fact is certain; speculation is futile.

As has been suggested, the teaching in the New Testament regarding Christ's coming is associated with appeals to faithfulness, with the enforcement of present duties, and with assurances that God's purposes will be accomplished. The Son of man commands all history, and it is working toward the accomplishment of God's purpose. He is guiding, ruling, overruling, and he will triumph over evil and bring his work to a glorious consummation, by the mighty power of redeeming love.

He is not coming to set up a kingdom here on this earth. He already has a kingdom, and it will "be delivered up to the Father" when Jesus comes. Then will be ushered in, not a thousand years' reign, but an eternal kingdom.

Concerning the time—nothing is more certain as to fact, but nothing more uncertain as to time. Nor man nor angel can tell. Only God himself knows. After all, what does it matter to us, when He is coming, whether at the first watch, at midnight, or at early dawn? "Watch therefore; for ye know not what hour your Lord doth come" (Matt. 24:42).

WHAT WILL TAKE PLACE AT HIS COMING?

The questions concerning the events of Christ's future coming have been answered briefly, insofar as the facts are revealed to us in the Bible. Beyond that, one dares not speak.

Christ comes again for the completion of his redemptive purpose, as has already been stressed. Neither his coming again nor any of the accompanying events are to be thought of in any arbitrary way, but each part as necessary to the completion of Christ's purpose. The resurrection of the dead, the judgment, the destruction of the present earth and heavens, and the coming of a new heaven and new earth—all are necessary adjuncts of this purpose.

The Resurrection

"There shall be a resurrection of the dead, both of the just and unjust" (Acts 24:15). When he comes "every eye shall see him" (Rev. 1:7). This includes the wicked. The idea of two physical resurrections, one of the righteous and another of the wicked a thousand years later, as premillennialism teaches, is without scriptural basis.

Christ himself said, "Marvel not at this: for the

hour is coming, in which all that are in the graves shall hear his voice, and shall come forth; they that have done good, unto the resurrection of life; and they that have done evil, unto the resurrection of damnation" (John 5:28-29).

The "first resurrection" spoken of in the Bible is a spiritual resurrection, which takes place at the time of the "new birth" when new life is given. "Blessed and holy is he that hath part in the first resurrection; on such the second death hath no power" (Rev. 20:6). The first resurrection is that spoken of in John 5:25, "The hour is coming and now is, when the dead shall hear the voice of the Son of God: and they that hear shall live." It is the passing "from death unto life," spoken of in I John 3:14.

The "second" or bodily resurrection is at the end of time, and is for the redemption of our bodies as set forth in Romans 8:23, when "this mortal must put on immortality" (I Cor. 15:53).

The Judgment

Following the resurrection there will be a general judgment: "It is appointed unto man once to die, but after this the judgment." Christ will "judge the quick and the dead at his appearing" (II Tim. 4:1). "When the Son of man shall come in his glory, and all the holy angels with him, then shall he sit upon the throne of his glory: and before him shall be gathered all nations: and he shall separate them one from another, as a shepherd divideth his sheep from the goats" (Matt. 25:31-32).

The Fate of the Lost

Those not redeemed or saved are spoken of as the lost. For at heart God's universe is a moral universe, and sin brings its own judgment. The judgments of God are not arbitrary, but are the judgments which sin of itself inevitably brings. The future brings to completion that which has begun here.

Men that are lost are men out of place. Man's rightful relationship to God is fellowship with God. God is now redeeming men. One day he will judge man. He offers life, but to those who will not have life, only death—spiritual death—remains.

There is eternal existence for the wicked, but it is existence apart from God. Whatever else hell may mean it means that place where God is not. Whatever else it may mean of separation, of isolation, of fire, of outer darkness, it means most of all, existence apart from God—lostness.

Such a concept of the future ought to bring to everyone a sense of the seriousness of the present and of accountability to the Judge of the universe. God now brings to bear all the influences he can upon men to get them to turn to him and be saved. If they will not, then only judgment is possible. And we can rest assured that God's judgments will be just, based upon the responsibility and accountability of the person, and His own holy sovereignty.

The Reward of the Saved

Could anything less than heaven be a fitting climax to such a redemptive purpose and plan as we have been studying? Heaven means the vast society of perfect persons capable of fellowship with God and with each other, where all shall "know even as also we are known."

This is the ultimate of God's saving grace—salvation. "He that endureth to the end shall be saved" (Matt. 10:22).

Heaven means the "many mansions" of Jesus. Heaven means home.

Several years ago I wrote in *Toward Understanding God*, "There is no virtue or need in trying to be abstract or exact in forming or stating our concept of heaven, nor is there any excuse for a writer to utter dull prosaics, when that which is in the Bible is anything but prosaic. So a writer had better refrain from writing than to be anything but poetic or imaginative, and that puts me in something of a corner. For I would like to write about heaven, but I am not poetic enough. But I can call to mind some of the beautiful symbols under which it is pictured in the Bible, and within the narrow limits of our mind we can at least consider some of the indefinable concepts of the spiritual ideal, such as white throne, white robes, pearly gates, golden streets, stately mansions, no sin, no sickness, no death, no tears, no night, no need of sun, etc. But why not look at the picture as painted by one who saw in panorama the scene pass before him and wrote:

"'After this I beheld, and lo, a great multitude, which no man could number, of all nations, and kindreds, and people, and tongues, stood before the throne, and before the Lamb, clothed with white robes, and palms in their hands; and cried with a loud voice, saying, Salvation to our God which sitteth upon the throne, and unto the Lamb. And all the angels stood round about the throne, and about the elders and the four beasts, and fell before the throne on their faces, and worshiped God, saying, Amen: Blessing, and glory, and wisdom, and thanksgiving, and honor, and power, and might, be unto our God forever and ever. Amen. And one of the elders answered, saying unto me, What are these which are arrayed in white robes? and whence came they? And I said unto him, Sir, thou

Concerning the Assured Hope of the Future 111

knowest. And he said to me, These are they which came out of great tribulation, and have washed their robes, and made them white in the blood of the Lamb. Therefore are they before the throne of God, and serve him day and night in his temple: and he that sitteth on the throne shall dwell among them. They shall hunger no more, neither thirst any more; neither shall the sun light on them, nor any heat. For the Lamb which is in the midst of the throne shall feed them, and shall lead them unto living fountains of waters: and God shall wipe away all tears from their eyes'" (Rev. 7:9-17).

SUMMING UP

Thinking back over our course of study in which we have tried to comprehend the entire sweep of God's redemptive purpose in Christ Jesus, we want to say again, All this and more we believe; all this and more we proclaim.

"In the beginning God" and his creation—in the end God and his new creation in eternal fellowship. All that has come and is yet to come in between has concerned us.

Possibly a recalling of the chapter headings will remind us again of the great scope of Christian belief. Possibly a looking into our own hearts will remind us again of our great privilege of proclaiming the gospel to others.

For if "this we believe" then it must inevitably follow "this we proclaim," for "out of the heart are the issues of life."

The purpose of our study, if we have properly grasped it, has not been just to get us to believe in God and these other items of Christian belief and there let the matter rest. It has been to challenge us to believe both that "God was in Christ, reconciling the world unto himself" and that therefore we should become heralds of that fact, beseeching men "in Christ's stead, be ye reconciled to God."

CPSIA information can be obtained at www.ICGtesting.com
Printed in the USA
BVOW030243300312

286460BV00006B/2/A